The Drumset Owner's Manual

For my parents,
Kathleen and George Vaughan.

The Drumset Owner's Manual

A Heavily Illustrated Guide to Selecting, Setting Up and Maintaining All Components of the Acoustic Drumset

by
Ronald Vaughan, 1952 –

McFarland & Company, Inc., Publishers
Jefferson, North Carolina, and London

British Library Cataloguing-in-Publication data are available

Library of Congress Cataloguing-in-Publication Data

Vaughan, Ronald, 1952–
    The drumset owner's manual : a heavily illustrated guide to
selecting, setting up and maintaining all components of the acoustic
drumset / by Ronald Vaughan.
    p. cm.
    Includes index.
    ISBN 0-89950-755-7 (sewn softcover : 55# alk. paper) ∞
    1. Drum — Maintenance and repair. 2. Drum — Purchasing. I. Title.
ML1035.V38 1993
786.9 — dc20   92-50323
                                                  CIP
                                               MN

Manufactured in the United States of America

McFarland & Company, Inc., Publishers
 Box 611, Jefferson, North Carolina 28640

Contents

Acknowledgments

When I started to write this book in the autumn of 1988, I didn't realize how long it would take and how many people would eventually assist me in one way or another. My research has put me in touch with so many individuals in the drumming world that it would be impossible to thank them all individually.

I'd like to express my appreciation to my fellow drummers and drum students whose ideas and questions during more than 20 years of teaching inspired me to write *The Drumset Owner's Manual*.

Being photographically inept, I was lucky to have the services of photographer and fellow drummer John Comber for the photos illustrating drum maintenance.

During the writing of *The Drumset Owner's Manual*, I contacted more than 100 companies that manufacture or distribute percussion equipment, requesting sales literature, photographs, product samples and technical information about their products. From that large number of letters and telephone calls, the following companies took the time to respond with useful material and information. The people at some of these companies went out of their way to be helpful. To those individuals, I offer a special thank you and my apologies for not being able to list your names. In all cases, I'm grateful to these companies for their assistance, support and enthusiasm for this book. They are, in alphabetical order:

Ace Products
35 Stillman Place, #201
San Francisco CA 94107

Avedis Zildjian Company
Longwater Dr.
Norwell MA 02061

Aquarian Accessories Corporation
1140 N. Tustin Ave.
Anaheim CA 92807

Beyerdynamic Inc.
5-05 Burns Ave.
Hicksville NY 11801

Corder Drum Company
3122 12th Ave. S.W.
Huntsville AL 35805

Danmar Percussion Products
7618 Woodman Ave.
Van Nuys CA 91402

The Drum Guys
16220 Territorial Rd.
Osseo MN 55369

Drum Workshop Inc.
2697 Lavery Ct., Unit 16
Newbury Park CA 91320

GMS Drum Company, Inc.
21 Louis St.
Hickville NY 11801

Gold Star Systems Ltd. Custom
    Flight Cases
344 Edgeley Blvd.
Concord, Ontario
Canada L4K 4B7

H. & A. Selmer Ltd.
95 Norfinch Dr.
Downsview, Ontario
Canada M3N 1W8

Impact Industries Inc.
333 Plumer St.
Wausau WI 54401

J.D. Calato Manuf. Co., Inc.
4501 Hyde Park Blvd.
Niagara Falls NY 14305

Korg U.S.A. Inc.
89 Frost St.
Westbury NY 11590

Latin Percussion Inc.
160 Belmont Ave.
Garfield NJ 07026

L. T. Lug Lock Inc.
P.O. Box 204
Tonawanda NY 14151

Ludwig Industries
Div. of the Selmer Company, L.P.
P.O. Box 310
Elkhart IN 46515-0310

Mike Balter Mallets
P.O. Box 531
Northbrook IL 60062

Neary Industries Ltd.
32 Academy St.
Kentville, Nova Scotia
Canada B4N 1S4

Noble & Cooley Drum Company
Water St.
Granville MA 01034

Paiste America, Inc.
460 Atlas St.
Brea CA 92621

Pro-Mark Corporation
10707 Craighead Dr.
Houston TX 77025

Purecussion Inc.
5957 West 37th St.
Minneapolis MN 55416

Rainbow Musical Products
20 Rainbow Pond Dr.
Suite A-2
Walpole MA 02081

Remo Inc.
12804 Raymer St.
North Hollywood CA 91605

Rimshot America
6454 Van Nuys Blvd., Suite 150
Van Nuys CA 91401

Roadrunner Cases, Inc.
447 E. Gardena Blvd.
Gardena CA 90248

R.O.C. Musical Instruments
64 Dorman
San Francisco CA 94124

Rota-Tip Drum Stick Company
P.O. Box 50
Milford MA 01757

Sabian Ltd. Cymbal Makers
Meductic, New Brunswick
Canada E0H 1L0

Shellkey
6925 Fifth Ave., Suite E122
Scottsdale AZ 85251

Shure Brothers Inc.
222 Hartrey Ave.
Evanston IL 60202

Timeline Products
P.O. Box 7611
Vallejo CA 94590

Trueline Drumstick Company
3610 Hancock St.
San Diego CA 92110

Ultimate Support Systems
P.O. Box 470
Fort Collins CO 80522-4700

Vic Firth Inc.
323 Whiting Ave., Unit B
Dedham MA 02026

If I've inadvertently missed any companies who should be on this list, I apologize.

The information in *The Drumset Owner's Manual* has been compiled from a multitude of sources. Much of it reached me in the form of tips that have been handed down over the years from drummer to drummer. I don't claim credit for discovering these ideas and I pass them along in the same spirit of fellowship. I also don't claim to have said the last word on the subject. Deciding what to include and what to leave out was one of the more difficult aspects of the project. If the information and opinions expressed in this book stimulate discussion and controversy, I think that's healthy.

Writing a book does involve some responsibility, though, and the blame for any errors or omissions is mine.

Ronald Vaughan

Introduction

If you buy an acoustic drumset (or any component of it), there is usually no owner's manual. You are expected to know how to set it up, how to tune it and how to maintain it in good condition. There are many excellent books on the subject of how to play drums, but there has been no comprehensive handbook about the drumset itself. Consequently, there are many fine drummers with years of playing experience who do not know much about their instrument.

That is why I wrote this book. The information covered by *The Drumset Owner's Manual* is a necessary part of every drummer's education. The book is designed to be easily understood by the novice and to be informative for the professional drummer. It is structured to build your knowledge in a step-by-step fashion and repetition of related information has been kept to a minimum. For this reason, you will derive the maximum benefit by reading the entire book in sequence rather than skipping immediately to a section that particularly interests you.

If you are considering the purchase of new equipment, *The Drumset Owner's Manual* can help you decide which features are important to you. If you are buying used equipment, the book will also show you what to look for to determine its condition. If you already own a drumset, you will learn logical methods for setting it up and tuning it to your taste. *The Drumset Owner's Manual* is packed with tips and ideas that can make your drumset sound better, look better and last longer.

Drumming instructors should be sure that all of their students have a copy of this book. School music teachers who aren't percussionists will find it to be a useful reference for selecting, setting up, tuning and caring for the drumsets in their schools.

The Drumset Owner's Manual can save you money by teaching you simple, inexpensive maintenance procedures that will keep your equipment functioning properly for years. This can also pay off when the time comes to sell or trade in your drumset, since well maintained drums, cymbals and hardware are worth much more on the used market than dirty, broken, neglected equipment.

There is a lack of standardized terminology among drummers. I have often heard the same word used by different people to refer to completely different parts of a drum. Conversely, the same part may be known by two or three different names. To minimize confusion to the reader, I've attempted to use the most descriptive, easily understood terms on a consistent basis throughout this book. Sometimes this entailed arbitrary choices of terms and you will undoubtedly continue to use the terminology with which you are most familiar.

You will find frequent reference to specific manufacturers or specific products throughout the book. In most cases, I have done this to point out a design feature and provide a concrete example of the feature that I am explaining. It is not necessarily meant to be an endorsement of the product. There may be other, similar products available of equal quality. I have my preferences in drum equipment (as we all do) and I do have endorsement agreements with several manufacturers. However, I have tried to be objective and to make it clear when I am voicing my opinion in addition to reporting facts. Lack of response from many manufacturers has prevented me from featuring an even wider selection of products in the book.

The drumset is a relatively new instrument that is constantly evolving in response to new musical styles and technological developments. This is particularly apparent in the electronics field. *The Drumset Owner's Manual* was written to fill a gap in percussion education literature on the subject of acoustic drumsets. Electronic drums, drum machines and related equipment are not included. Their more rapid rate of change would make information about them outdated long before the book could be published.

The best way to keep up to date with what is new in drumming both acoustically and electronically is to read the various drum magazines regularly. You will find new product test reports, interviews with top drummers and articles on various aspects of performance. You will also find advertisements with the addresses of manufacturers where you can write for catalogs and price lists. Be the best drummer you can be by staying well informed.

Low quality equipment or badly maintained equipment is a hindrance to the drummer. High quality equipment that is properly tuned and maintained can inspire a drummer to play well and enjoy the experience of making music. *The Drumset Owner's Manual* can show you how to get the most from your drumset. The rest is up to you.

Drum Basics

The drums used in most acoustic drumsets have certain features in common. In basic terms, they are cylinders with membranes (sheets of thin material) stretched across the ends. The cylinder is called a drumshell. The membrane is called a drumhead. Striking the head produces the sound.

The dimensions of the shell determine the potential range of pitch a drum can produce. The larger the diameter and or depth of shell, the lower the pitch. The smaller the diameter and or depth of shell, the higher the pitch. For this reason, drumshells are manufactured in a range of sizes for different purposes.

Materials and Construction of Drumshells

The material and construction of the shell affects the tonal quality of the drum's sound. Most shells are made of wood or metal. Wood fiber, fiberglass and acrylic plastic are also used. Combinations such as wood lined with fiberglass have been tried. Each material has its own construction methods and contributes its own acoustic properties to the finished shell.

The majority of wood drumshells are made from plywood. In the more traditional construction method, a thin sheet of plywood is bent into a cylindrical shape and the ends are tapered and glued together to form a lap joint. To strengthen the shell and retain its shape, wooden reinforcement rings are glued inside each end of the cylinder. Although this type of plywood construction used to be very common, it is no longer used by many manufacturers.

Currently, most plywood drumshells are constructed in a mold. Each ply is shaped in the mold and the ends are butt jointed. Successive plies are glued in place with the butt joint of each ply offset from the last. The

1

absence of a single lap joint creates a strong shell with uniform thickness and no single weak point. These shells are usually thick enough to maintain their shape without reinforcement rings.

Some drumshells are manufactured from solid wood instead of plywood. Thin sheets of wood are either dry or steam-bent, lap jointed and fitted with reinforcement rings, much like the construction method described earlier. Noble & Cooley is one company using this type of solid wood construction.

The most common materials used for metal shells are steel, aluminum, brass and bronze. In the usual method of construction, a machine presses a thin sheet of metal into shape. Flanges at each end of the shell provide a smooth edge (for head tensioning) and rigidity to help the shell maintain its round shape. Some metal shells have a welded seam running from one end of the cylinder to the other. This is where the metal was joined together after shaping. Other shells are drawn and spun, producing a seamless cylindrical piece of metal that is shaped into a shell. Less common is cast metal construction, where the drumshell is cast in one piece and then machined and polished to smooth rough edges and finish its appearance. The cast bronze shell Signature Series snare drums from Sonor are examples of this construction method.

Wood fiber and fiberglass drumshells are produced by laminating wood fibrous material or fiberglass cloth in a mold or around a mandrel. Resins are used to harden this material into a solid mass. This produces a strong shell requiring no reinforcement rings. The Acousticon shells of Remo drums are a wood fiber and resin composite material, while Impact is an example of a company manufacturing fiberglass shell drums. Transparent acrylic plastic drumshells, which were popular during the early 1970s, are also molded. They require no reinforcement rings, but often have a seam running from one edge to the other which can be a weak point. The (now obsolete) Ludwig Vista-Lite series of drums were an example of transparent acrylic shell construction.

Acoustic Properties of Drumshells

The material and construction of the shell has an effect on the tonal quality of the drum, although this effect is minor when compared to the contribution of the drumhead. Variables that affect the tonal quality of drumshells include shell material, internal finish of shell material and thickness of shell.

Before making generalizations about the acoustic effects of each variable, it is important to point out that isolating each factor is difficult.

Other aspects of a drum's construction and finish will enhance or moderate the effect of any one design specification. You hear the end result; differences are subtle in most cases.

Regardless of the material used, a thin shell vibrates more easily than a thick shell when the head is struck. Thick, heavy shells are more acoustically inert than thin shells. In general, a thick shell will be perceived as brighter sounding with more high overtones. A thin shell will sound warmer, producing more low overtones. It is possible to over-play a thin shell drum, causing it to sound choked. Conversely, thick

Cross section of Ludwig drumshell, showing plywood construction with bevelled bearing edge and no reinforcement rings. *(Courtesy of Ludwig.)*

shell drums react more fully when played louder. The characteristics of thick or thin shells are similar to hard or soft shells, respectively, as explained below. This is because a thicker shell is "harder" or more resistant to vibration than a thin shell.

Shell material affects the sound of a drum according to its relative hardness or softness. This is further influenced by the internal finish of the shell. Rigid material with a smooth, non-porous surface reflects more of the full range of frequencies generated by striking the drumhead. Softer, more elastic and porous material absorbs some frequencies and reflects others, slightly altering the resulting sound. A drum with a full range of overtones is described as bright and resonant. A drum with fewer overtones is described as warm and mellow.

Metal is the hardest material commonly used in shell construction. It reflects the greatest range of vibrations. This gives metal shell drums their characteristic bright, ringy sound. They reflect the higher frequencies that softer materials partially absorb. Minor differences in the acoustic properties of different metals are due to their relative degree of hardness. Brass, bronze or aluminum shells are softer than steel, giving them a warmer sound that is slightly less harsh than steel. Shell thickness and chrome or other plating will emphasize or minimize this characteristic.

Fiberglass and acrylic shells are softer than metal, but less porous than wood, giving them a degree of brightness in between that of metal and wood. Fiberglass shells sometimes have a textured inner surface, while acrylic shells are usually smooth inside and out. This less reflective surface can give fiberglass drums more warmth than acrylic drums, all other factors being equal. Interesting to note are the Acousticon wood fiber shells manufactured by Remo, Inc. The interiors of these shells are purposely sealed with resins to obtain the desired degree of harmonic reflection and absorption.

Wood is the softest material commonly used in shells. In its natural state, it absorbs the greatest range of frequencies. Wood shells are more mellow sounding than metal or synthetic shells. Many types of wood have been used for drumshells. The most common at this time are maple, birch and mahogany, either alone or in combination. The relative hardness and porosity of different woods gives them different acoustic properties. Generally, the harder the wood, the brighter the sound and the softer the wood, the warmer the sound. However, most wood shells are coated inside with paint, varnish or a similar sealant to prevent moisture absorption and warpage. The thickness and porosity of the sealant alters the wood's ability to absorb frequencies to a greater or lesser extent. Each manufacturer has its own materials and methods. This makes valid comparisons between the acoustic properties of specific types of wood very difficult.

You can get an idea of the resonance of a shell by putting your head inside it and talking or by striking the shell with a drumstick. Experiment with shells of different materials and interior finishes, listening for the presence or absence of high pitched echo. High quality shell construction will mean more in practical terms to most drummers than a specific shell material. Your ears will tell you if the drum has the tonal quality you want.

Drumshell Finishes

Just as the interiors of some shells are finished or coated, so are the exteriors. Before the widespread use of transparent drumheads, interior finishes were applied primarily to prevent moisture absorption in wood shells. Little thought was given to the appearance of the inside of the shell. Now the inside of a wooden drumshell may be stained or varnished in the same way as the exterior, with much consideration given to the cosmetic value of such an operation.

The exterior finish of a drumshell has several functions. It must prevent moisture absorption in wood shells or tarnish and corrosion in metal shells. It must also provide some degree of durability against bumps and scratches during the use and transport of the drum. But of course, the exterior finish is designed primarily to look good. There are several types of exterior shell finishes.

Metal shells are often chrome plated to prevent rust or tarnish in addition to improving their appearance. Unplated shells made from brass or bronze are sometimes coated with clear lacquer to preserve their shine. Older metal drums were sometimes plated with nickel, but this requires more frequent polishing than chrome to keep it shiny. It is rarely used these days.

Transparent acrylic plastic shells require no exterior or interior finish. Their appearance was the main reason for their popularity for a few years. The exteriors of fiberglass shells are usually painted for cosmetic reasons, fiberglass, like acrylic, being moisture proof.

Most wooden shells are finished in one of three ways. The first method is called a wood grain finish. The shell is stained and then sealed with transparent lacquer, leaving the grain of the wood visible and highlighted like a piece of wooden furniture. A variety of stains are available to create eye catching colors or natural wood finishes.

The second method is called a lacquer finish. The shell is coated with an opaque, colored paint, leaving a smooth, glossy surface with no wood grain visible. Plain or pearlescent colors are used. It should be noted that the term "lacquer" in wood grain or painted finishes may not be technically correct. This is the traditional expression, but modern drumshell finishes may consist of other types of paint or varnish.

The third method is called a plastic wrap finish. It was once known as a "pearl" finish (which was unrelated to the drum manufacturer of that name), since the early plastic finishes were patterned like the inside of sea shells. A thin sheet of colored plastic material is glued to the exterior of the shell. Plastic finishes include plain colors, metal flake sparkles, mirrored chrome, the original marine pearls and other patterns. There is a wide variety of plastic finishes available for re-covering older drums or custom-finishing a new drumset.

Certain exterior finishes go in and out of fashion, sometimes returning to popularity with a new generation of drummers. In recent years, the trend has been away from plastic finishes. However, signs are beginning to show that this trend is reversing.

Proponents of wood grain and lacquer finishes say that the addition of a layer of plastic to the exterior of a drumshell inhibits the shell's resonance. This sounds logical in theory and may be a factor for extremely thin shell drums. However, although the difference in resonance may be measurable in an acoustic laboratory, there is no appreciable difference in practice. My skepticism is furthered by the tendency of some manufacturers to use massive tuning hardware on their wood grain or lacquer shells. The resonance muffling effect of this hardware would certainly offset any extra resonance gained by the absence of a plastic wrap finish.

The durability of a drum's finish must be considered because it eventually affects the drum's appearance and value. Wood grain and lacquer shells must be treated very carefully to avoid cosmetic damage. The finish will chip or scratch fairly easily. This damage shows up clearly and is difficult to repair. Additionally, fluctuating temperature and humidity levels can cause minute cracks in the finish due to expansion and contraction of the wood.

Plastic finishes are not as delicate and do not show wear as quickly. The best plastic finishes for obscuring small nicks and scratches are the marine pearls, sparkles or other patterned finishes that break up the smooth expanse of a single color. Plastic has its drawbacks, however. White or light colored plastics may turn yellow with age. Black or dark colored plastics can develop ripples in their surface if exposed to extreme heat or direct sunlight for very long (light colors retain less heat and are less likely to develop this problem). Mirror chrome plastics are so smooth and reflective that nicks and scratches show up easily.

Any type of dark finish shows every speck of dust and requires daily dusting if not covered. Although there are many pros and cons, most drummers just buy the one they like the appearance of.

Bearing Edges

The bearing edge is the term used to describe the edge of the drumshell at each end of the cylinder. The drumhead contacts the drumshell at this point. As its name implies, this is the bearing surface over which the head is tensioned. If this area is smooth and evenly formed, the drum should tune easily. If it is rough, warped, or uneven in any way, there can be friction, unpleasant overtones and tuning difficulties. A sufficiently rough bearing edge could even puncture a drumhead. Unfortunately, this part of the shell sometimes receives less attention than it deserves during the manufacturing process.

The way a bearing edge is shaped effects the sound of the drum. More shell material in contact with the underside of the head has a slight muffling effect, leading to fewer overtones and shorter sustain. Less shell material touching the head allows it to vibrate more freely, creating more overtones and longer sustain. Many older drums have wide, rounded bearing edges,

Impact seven-piece fiberglass shell drumset with single-headed toms cut away at front to increase projection. Also notice large vent holes in toms and bass drumshell to increase projection and allow insertion of microphones. *(Courtesy of Impact.)*

while the current trend is to narrow, sharp bearing edges. As with other areas of shell construction, there is no right or wrong configuration. Precise leveling and uniform shaping of the bearing edge is more important to good sound quality than any specific amount of width or sharpness of angle.

Vent Holes

Most double headed drums (those with drumheads at both ends of the drumshell) have one or more vent holes to allow air to escape when the head is depressed by striking. The vent hole is usually located at the midpoint of the shell depth. Some older drums (for example, some Gretsch drums manufactured prior to 1971) have no vent hole at all. The Noble & Cooley Drum Company locates vent holes near the bottom of the shell depth to allow the complete air column inside the shell to be set in motion before being vented. The Ludwig slotted Coliseum snare drum has an upper and lower shell with a significant gap between them instead of the usual vent hole. This is to maximize volume and sound projection. Similarly, the fiberglass shell drums made by Impact have extremely large vent holes that also allow the insertion of microphones into the shell.

The edge of the vent hole is covered by a metal grommet for cosmetic reasons. Often, this grommet becomes the means for securing the manufacturer's trademark badge to the shell. Other than the previously mentioned slotted drum, the most significant difference in sound quality due to venting appears in extremely shallow shells. When the drumheads are no more than three or four inches apart and the drum is struck hard, additional (or larger) vent holes help to prevent the drum from sounding choked. Some manufacturers include such additional vent holes in various sizes of shells to optimize venting.

Tuning Hardware

All drums use some type of hardware to tighten the drumheads over the ends of the shells. Old military marching drums used wooden counterhoops tensioned by ropes. Inexpensive bongo drums can still be found with heads tacked directly to the shell.

Modern drums use counterhoops to hold the head in place. The counterhoop derives its name from its function. It fits over the "hoop" that forms the perimeter of the drumhead. Tension rods around the counterhoop thread into tension casings, pulling the counterhoop down and stretching the head across the end of the shell. Wooden counterhoops are still used on most bass drums. Other drums use metal counterhoops, either pressed steel or die cast. Modern, triple flanged, pressed steel counterhoops are the result of several design innovations over the years.

Early metal counterhoops were similar in design to the wooden ones still used on bass drums. Claw hooks grasped the straight edge of the counterhoop. Tension rods pulled the claw hooks to tune the head. By adding a flange at the bottom of the counterhoop, then extending this flange outward and drilling holes or slots in it for the tension rods, claw hooks were eliminated. Without the claw hooks, the upper edge of the counterhoop did not have to be straight. It was flanged inward or outward to create a smoother, rounder edge that is much less destructive to drumsticks.

Pressed steel counterhoops can bend or warp out of shape if they receive too much tension at any one point. Some manufacturers use pressed counterhoops made from a heavier gauge of steel to minimize this problem.

Die cast counterhoops are thicker, heavier and stronger. Cast metal is

Ludwig triple-flanged hoop *(below)* and die-cast hoop *(above)* illustrating difference in construction. *(Courtesy of Ludwig.)*

more resistant to bending or warping than pressed metal. This makes die cast counterhoops a good solution for high tension applications. They are more costly and their rigidity can be a drawback, however. If you are trying to tune a drum with an uneven edge or an unevenly seated head, a die cast counterhoop cannot flex to accommodate it.

The place most likely to break on either type of counterhoop is the area surrounding the holes or slots for the tension rods. This is where it receives the greatest stress. Some recent designs of die cast counterhoops attempt to address this problem by casting an extended bottom flange all the way around the counterhoop. Holes for the tension rods are drilled through this continuous, thick flange instead of through the small, projecting "ears" used on older designs. This adds weight and bulk to the counterhoop, but reduces the manufacturing cost. One casting can now be used for each shell diameter, with the appropriate number of holes drilled for the specific application.

Some manufacturers fit die cast counterhoops on all their drums. Most fit them or offer them as options only for high tension and potential heavy abuse applications such as snare drums. It is unlikely that any other drum on the set will be tensioned high enough to really need the extra strength of die cast counterhoops. Depending on your style of playing and the amount of tension you use, you may not require them at all.

The construction of a drum's counterhoop also has an effect on the sound of the drum. Most noticeable when playing rim shots (when simultaneously striking the drumhead with the tip of the drumstick and the counterhoop with the shaft of the drumstick), die cast or pressed steel counterhoops contribute different acoustic effects. In the same way that thin drumshells vibrate more freely and thick drumshells vibrate less freely, the lighter, pressed steel counterhoop gives a bright, ringy rim shot, while the heavier, die cast counterhoop gives a drier rim shot with shorter sustain.

The use of pressed steel counterhoops rather than wooden counterhoops on some bass drums also affects the sound. Metal counterhoops give

Sonor Signature series snare drum with parallel-action throw-off. Notice the round headed, slotted tension rods. *(Courtesy of Korg U.S.A.)*

a bass drum slightly more ring and sustain, while wooden counterhoops are slightly less resonant. This effect is similar to the above-mentioned difference between pressed steel or die cast counterhoops on other drums. The choice of counterhoop material and construction should be based on personal preference.

Tension rods are threaded bolts that connect the counterhoop to the shell and regulate the tension of the drumhead. Most have a square head to fit a standard drum tuning key. Round headed, slotted styles are found on Sonor drums and older Premier drums. Different thread dimensions may be used by different manufacturers and different lengths of tension rods may be used by the same manufacturer on different drums, so tension rods are not necessarily interchangeable from one drum to another. A metal or nylon washer is fitted between the counterhoop and the head of the tension rod to smooth its rotation when tuning.

Bass drum tension rods often feature t-handles, which may be turned by hand, in place of the usual square heads. This is due to tradition rather than functional necessity, and you may prefer to replace the t-handle rods with normal, square headed ones. Most manufacturers now fit square headed tension rods on both sides of the spot where a bass drum pedal is clamped to the bass drum counterhoop. This is to prevent a large t-handle from interfering with the proper attachment of the pedal.

The tension rod threads into a tension casing, which is secured to the drumshell. There are several styles of hardware used in this application.

The most basic difference is between single tension and separate tension designs.

Although rarely seen now, some older, inexpensive drums had long tension rods reaching from one counterhoop to the other. Turning these rods pulled the counterhoops closer together, tensioning both drumheads at the same time. This lack of independent control over the tension of each head is called single tension. The hardware was simple and inexpensive, but that was its only advantage. Single tension drums are difficult to tune properly. No major manufacturer uses this system on modern drums designed for drumset application.

Separate tension, meaning the ability to tune each head independently, is a feature now taken for granted on even the least expensive, entry-level drum. Tension rods from each counterhoop thread into separate rows of tension casings or into opposite ends of a centrally located row of tension casings.

The choice of whether to use a single or double row of tension casings is usually determined by the depth of the shell. Shallow drumshells do not have room for two rows unless they are offset from each other. Deep shells would require extremely long tension rods to reach a centrally located tension casing.

Until the 1970s, several manufacturers offered lower priced drumsets featuring a single, centrally located row of tension casings on each drum, regardless of shell depth. Using less hardware kept the price down, but the extremely long tension rods used on the deeper shells were vulnerable to damage and often bent, making precise tuning difficult. This is another design rarely seen now.

Another way in which price is still kept low on inexpensive drums is by limiting the number of tension casings and tension rods around each head. In general, the more points there are around the head of a drum at which the tension is applied, the more precise the tuning can be. This holds true up to a point. To use a 14″ diameter snare drum as an example, it is possible to find inexpensive models with only six tension points around each head. By the 1960s, professional quality models always used at least eight tension points. The better models had ten tension points to achieve even more precise control over even head tension. By the 1970s, manufacturers such as Slingerland were offering models with 12 tension points around each head. To go much further would drive up the cost of the drum while achieving little or no noticeable improvement to sound. The same logic applies to bass drums and toms. For drums fitted with die cast counterhoops that are resistant to flexing, using more than a standard number of tuning points would be even less beneficial.

Separate rows of tension casings for each head can place great stress

GMS drumset. Notice the tubular tension casings which swivel to make them self-aligning. *(Courtesy GMS Drum Co.)*

on the drumshell in high tension applications. The more tension applied, the more the casing tries to pull away from the shell. The thinner the shell, the greater is the danger. On a shallow shell with a centrally located row of casings, the opposing tension of the two heads relieves much of this stress on the shell. Some manufacturers have adapted this concept to deeper shells by using long, double ended casings on all their drums. In most instances, the amount of tension used does not justify a need for these high tension casings. They appear to be primarily a cosmetic consideration, but the idea is valid in true high tension applications.

Most tension casings are chrome plated metal castings. Every manufacturer uses a slightly different shape to make their drums identifiable even before you see a trademark name plate. Early tension casings were thin, internally threaded metal tubes with pieces projecting from their sides to bolt them to the shell. Some companies have returned to this older style of hardware, claiming that its minimal contact with the drum causes less interference with the resonance of a thin shell. Sonor Hilite series drums use this type of low mass hardware with the addition of rubber grommets at each attachment point to insulate its contact with the shell. The Pearl drum company has taken this concept to its limit by producing a range of Free Floating snare drums that have no hardware at all bolted to the shell. Experimentation will determine whether these design features make a significant difference in sound.

These tubular tension casings were phased out years ago when the now common self-aligning tension casing was developed. When you replace a head on a drum fitted with tubular tension casings, each tension rod must be precisely aligned with the internally threaded tube in order to avoid cross-threading. The development of a cast tension casing with a separate, threaded insert solved this problem. The threaded insert projects from the end of the tension casing, held in place by a spring that allows it to flex. This range of movement lets the insert align itself as the tension rod is threaded, minimizing the cross-threading problem and speeding up the installation of heads. The value of this feature can only be appreciated by trying to do without it. The GMS drum company appears to have developed a "best of both worlds" solution by using low mass, tubular casings that incorporate a swivel mechanism to aid in tension rod alignment.

Types of Drums

The three basic types of drums used in the acoustic drumset are bass drums, toms and snare drums. Within each type there are variations in size and design. The size of a drum is determined by exterior measurements of its bare shell, before the addition of heads or tuning hardware. Measurements in this book are given in inches, the first measurement being the depth of the shell and the second measurement being its diameter, for example 14″ × 22″.

Every drum has a batter head (the head that is struck). If a second head is used at the opposite end of the shell, it is called a resonator head. These terms are used to avoid any confusion about "top," "bottom," "front" or "back" heads. The one exception to this terminology is the resonator head designed for use on a snare drum, which is called a snare head.

Ludwig nine-piece double bass drumset. Notice the extra deep shell snare drum and the use of boom stands to place cymbals within reach. *(Courtesy of Ludwig.)*

Bass Drums

The bass drum, as its name suggests, is the bass or low pitched voice of the drumset. It rests on the floor with the surface of the heads in a vertical position so that it may be struck by the beater attached to a foot pedal.

The standard or conventional depth of a bass drumshell is 14″. Extended depth or "power" shells may be 16″ or 18″ deep, with some examples as deep as 24″. Standard shell diameters range from 18″ to 26″ in increments of two inches, with rare examples of 28″ or even 30″. During the history of the drumset, various bass drum sizes have been popular at different times. Lately, the most common sizes are 16″ depth × 22″ diameter or 14″ depth × 22″ diameter. Smaller bass drums of 14″ × 18″, 14″ × 20″ or 16″ × 20″ are often favored by jazz drummers. Larger bass drums of 16″ × 24″, 18″ × 24″ or 16″ × 26″ are often the choice of heavy rock drummers. In some cases, these choices are made for reasons of desired tonal quality or, additionally, in the case of small drums, to minimize size and weight for transport. In other cases, size is chosen for reasons of appearance according to what is currently fashionable.

During the 1970s, some companies made single headed bass drums. No hardware was fitted to allow the use of a resonator head. This design has gone out of fashion and most drummers now use a full or partial resonator head on their bass drums.

The basic drumset has one bass drum. Some drummers use two bass drums, often of the same size but occasionally of two different sizes. This allows them to play bass drum rhythms that are too fast or complex for one foot. The development of the double foot pedal, which allows both feet to play independently on one bass drum, has made it unnecessary for drummers to carry a second bass drum. However, some drummers still prefer the sound and feeling of separate bass drums, while others continue to use them for reasons of appearance.

Toms

Toms (originally known as tom-toms) are the melodic, mid-range voices of the drumset. They are played with sticks, brushes or mallets and may be mounted on stands, on a holder attached to the bass drum or on their own legs. The basic drumset at this time has three toms. Most drumsets have at least one or two toms and may have as many as nine.

The shell dimensions of toms vary from one manufacturer to another. Typically, diameters range from 6″ to 18″ in one or two inch increments. Shell depth generally increases as diameter increases. Smaller sizes attached to stands or holders are called mounted toms. Larger sizes supported on legs are called floor toms. This used to be a clear point of division, but larger toms are now sometimes mounted on stands, gaining the confusing designation of mounted floor toms.

At the same time that bass drums without resonator heads were popular, toms without resonator heads were also in fashion. These single headed drums are called concert toms. Their shells have no hardware for fitting resonator heads. Most drummers have returned to using toms with resonator heads.

Just as bass drumshells are currently made in conventional or extended depths, tom shells are available in extended or "power" depths. The resulting number of choices in conventional or extended depths is extensive.

The relationship of depth to diameter started with the 9″ × 13″ mounted tom and the 16″ × 16″ floor tom. These traditional sizes were reduced to 8″ × 12″ and 14″ × 14″ respectively for smaller drumsets. As drumsets grew and the range of available sizes expanded, shell diameters of 7″, 9″, 11″ and 17″ were avoided by most manufacturers. Shell depths

Ludwig five-piece drumset showing mounted toms with extended shell depth. *(Courtesy of Ludwig.)*

for the less traditional diameters of 6″, 8″, 10″ and 15″ have always varied from one manufacturer to another, while 14″ diameter toms settled on a shell depth of 10″.

The introduction of extended depth toms brought even more variance. Some manufacturers use a ratio of one or two inches less depth than diameter, such as 11″ × 13″ or 12″ × 13″ while others offer "square" dimension shells such as 13″ × 13″. Checking catalog specifications will show you what sizes are available from each manufacturer.

Before leaving the subject of toms, it is worth mentioning another variation. RotoToms were developed by Remo, Inc. and are now manufactured by several companies. They are single headed toms without shells in the normal sense of the word. Manufactured in several diameters, they consist of a metal casting (in place of a shell, to mount the head) and a counterhoop to tension the head. The casting is mounted on a threaded shaft which permits the tension and pitch of the head to be raised or lowered by spinning the RotoTom on the shaft. They are usually mounted on floor stands in groups of two or more and have become popular with some drummers as add-on toms for their drumset.

Snare Drums

The snare drum is the high pitched voice of the drumset, due to its unique construction. It is usually mounted on a stand and placed immediately in front of the drummer. The basic drumset has one snare drum and it is often regarded as the most important drum in the set.

GMS piccolo snare drum showing a shallow shell depth. *(Courtesy of GMS Drum Co.)*

The standard diameter for a snare drumshell is 14". Depths range from 3" to 10". Snare drums of less than 5" shell depth are now called piccolo snare drums, although a traditional piccolo snare drum also has a smaller diameter of 13". For many years, 5" was the standard depth for snare drums used on drumsets. During the 1970s and 1980s, the trend to deeper shells for all drums made 6½" the standard depth. Shells of 8" and 10" depth are often used by rock drummers and there has been a revival of interest in piccolo snare drums.

While a snare drumshell may be made from any of the usual materials, it is the only drum in the set that commonly has a metal shell.

The distinguishing feature of a snare drum that creates its characteristic sound is the set of snares tensioned across the resonator head or snare head as it is called. This snare head is quite thin, so it vibrates easily when the batter head is struck. These vibrations "rattle" the snares against the head, giving the snare drum a sharper, more piercing tonal quality than a bass drum or tom.

Most of the snares used on modern snare drums are made from lengths of coiled wire soldered or glued between end plates. The thinner the wire, the easier the snares vibrate. The thicker the wire, the more vibration is required to activate them. The number of wire strands used varies from 12 to 42. Occasionally, cable snares are used. These are constructed like guitar strings, with a central wire core wrapped in thin wire and soldered or glued to end plates.

Earlier snares were lengths of gut like the material used to string old-fashioned tennis rackets. Wire-wound gut was also used for a snappier sound. These individual gut strands were clamped in a snare butt at one side of the shell, running across the snare head to a snare strainer at the

Drum Workshop snare drums, showing variations in shell depth, shell material and single or double row tension casings. *(Courtesy of Drum Workshop.)*

other side. The snare strainer, which gets its name from the strain or tension it applies to the snares, was a simple bracket with a tension screw to tighten the snares. There was no provision for quickly engaging or disengaging the snares from the head.

A snare throw-off was eventually incorporated into the strainer tension screw device, allowing the drummer to play the drum with snares on or off at the flip of a lever. Some variation of this idea is used on all modern snare drums. With coiled wire snares, the snare unit is attached to the strainer and butt by means of cord, tape or plastic strips. This material passes through snare gates cut out of the snare head counterhoop.

In the simplest type of mechanism, the tension screw controls both the amount of lengthwise stretch applied to the snares and their degree of tension against the snare head. More sophisticated systems separate these two functions, allowing the drummer to adjust them independently and have more precise control over the resulting sound.

The easiest way to separate these functions is by the use of a bridge, like the bridge on a guitar or violin. The cord, tape or plastic strips exit the snare gates (holes or slots cut out of the resonator side counterhoop) at each side of the drum and are tensioned across bridges before reaching the strainer or butt. The bridges, which may be factory set or owner adjustable, determine how tightly the snares contact the snare head. The tension screw controls the amount of stretch applied to the snares. Snare throw-off mechanisms with bridges are used by several manufacturers.

Another method of achieving the same goal is used on the Rogers Dyna-Sonic snare drum. The wire snares are attached to a metal frame and tensioned on the frame. The frame is suspended below the snare head with the tension screw on the throw-off controlling the amount of snare contact with the head.

Top: Antique Ludwig snare drum, showing tubular tension casings, single flanged hoops with claw hooks and early parallel-action snare throw-off design. *Center:* Modern Ludwig snare drum, showing self-aligning tension casings, triple-flanged hoops and modern parallel-action snare throw-off. *Bottom:* Ludwig slotted Coliseum snare drum, showing slotted shell instead of vent hole and lock nuts on batter head tension rods to prevent de-tuning. *(Courtesy of Ludwig.)*

The parallel-action throw-off is another method used by several manufacturers. A thin rod passes across the interior of the drumshell, connecting the throw-off and butt mechanisms. When the throw-off lever is raised or lowered, the snares are lifted or dropped simultaneously at both ends. Each end of the mechanism has provision for adjusting the degree of snare contact with the head. The snares extend past the edge of the head at both ends to improve snare response when playing near the edges of the batter head. The snares are held in constant tension between the throw-off and the butt, with provision for tension adjustment at one or both ends. Parallel-action throw-offs often permit different snare units to be used, some with combinations of different types of snares and some, such as the optional units for the Ludwig Super-Sensitive models, with individually adjustable strands.

Like any mechanical device, these designs provide superior sound and snare response only if they are correctly adjusted. If you do not understand their intended function and method of operation, you will be better off with the basic throw-off mechanism.

In order to allow the snares to contact the snare head properly, the bearing edge of the snare drumshell is usually cut away at the two opposite points where the snares or their attachment material cross the shell. This area is called the snare bed. If you remove the snare head and examine the shell carefully, it is visible as two slight, gradual dips in the bearing edge. This is the only case where a variation in the bearing edge is not only acceptable, but necessary.

Drum Maintenance
and Selection

Care and Maintenance

Preventive maintenance can keep drums looking like new, functioning perfectly and sounding great for a lifetime. Neglect can destroy drums in a very short time. Whenever I buy a new or used drum, I dismantle it and give it a thorough cleaning, inspection, lubrication and adjustment. After that, periodic inspection and maintenance keep it in excellent condition.

Predicting the required frequency of maintenance procedures for all drums with accuracy is not possible. The environment in which you play or store your drums, their frequency of use and how hard you play them are all factors that influence their rate of wear and tear. Whatever amount of time you spend, it pays off. Things usually break in the middle of a performance, when it is most inconvenient. Regular inspection and maintenance can catch most problems before they cause such a disaster. Also, well maintained drums cost you less in broken, worn out and missing parts and they bring a higher resale price if you sell them.

The following pages describe a step by step procedure to put your drums in good shape. Read the instructions carefully and take your time. It may take you a few days to do every drum in your set but the results are worth the effort. Many of the procedures must be done only once, while others should be repeated when your inspections show that they are needed. Most of the work requires no particular mechanical skills but a few of the steps might be entrusted to a competent professional drum repair person if you do not feel confident about doing them yourself.

You will need a clean, well lit work area with table or work bench and a number of trays or boxes to keep the small parts organized as you take the drums apart. Some cleaning chemicals are flammable and some give off unhealthy fumes. Always check the labels on their containers for hazard warnings, take the necessary precautions to avoid accidents and work in a room with adequate ventilation. If your skin is sensitive to solvents, you may wish to wear rubber gloves. This can be a dirty job, especially if the drums are not new, so wear appropriate work clothing. Keep paper and pencil handy to make note of broken, worn out or missing parts as you work. A small selection of hand tools is needed. These will be mentioned as their use arises.

To do a thorough job, each drum must be disassembled to its component parts. When you have had some experience at this, you can disassemble all the drums at once and complete each procedure on every drum before going on to the next step. If you have no experience at taking drums apart (or more importantly, at putting them together), I advise you to complete each drum as a separate project. What looks very simple as you are removing pieces may turn into an unsolvable puzzle by the time you begin to reassemble the drum. Having another drum available that is still in one piece is very useful for purposes of comparison. Drawing diagrams that show the order and location of parts being removed can aid you in reassembly.

Start by covering your work bench or table with several layers of cloth or newspapers to avoid scratching the drum as you work. Have some clean, soft cloths handy for wiping dirty or greasy parts (and dirty or greasy hands).

1. Place the drum on your work table. Examine it carefully and make note of any obvious problems such as broken heads, broken snares on a snare drum, missing tension rods, etc. Start your list of parts requiring repair or replacement.

2. For snare drums only, turn the drum snare side up and remove the snares. This may require an appropriate screwdriver or drum tuning key to loosen the clamping points at the strainer and butt. Handle coiled wire snare units carefully to avoid bending the strands. Place the snares in a box or parts tray, allowing them to lie flat.

3. Turn the drum so that the batter head faces up. Fit your drum tuning key on one of the tension rods and turn it counter-clockwise one full turn. This loosens the tension on the head. Move the key from one tension rod to the next, loosening one full turn. When you have loosened each tension rod several times, there should be no tension left in the head.

4. Remove one tension rod at a time by continuing to unscrew them. Place the tension rods in a parts tray. There should be a metal or nylon washer under the head of each tension rod. Make note of any missing washers.

5. Lift the counterhoop off the head. Wipe off any loose dust or dirt, examine it for rust, peeling chrome or other obvious damage and place it in a parts tray.

Removing the hoop and head. *(Courtesy John Comber.)*

6. Lift the head off the shell. Wipe off the dust and dirt that collects around the edge, examine it to determine its condition and place it in a parts tray.

7. If the drum is double headed, turn it over and repeat steps 3 to 6 for the resonator head.

8. Remove the tension casings from the shell. They are bolted to the shell from the inside. Select the appropriate screwdriver, nut driver or socket wrench. Each screw or bolt should have a spring lock washer under it to prevent it from loosening and a large washer under that to spread the stress over a larger area. Make note of any missing or broken parts. Don't lose any springs or threaded inserts that may be inside the tension casings. Occasionally a spring will pop out as a tension casing is removed from the shell. Put all this hardware in a parts tray.

9. Remove any other hardware, such as internal tone controls, mounting brackets, snare butt or strainer on snare drums. This will also require an appropriate screwdriver, nut driver or socket wrench. Place these items in a parts tray.

10. Examine the bare shell inside and out for cracks in the shell material, damage to the interior or exterior finish, delamination of wood plies, etc. Serious shell damage requires replacement of the shell or the

entire drum. Minor prob-
lems can sometimes be
repaired with glue on wood
shells or with fiberglass
repair material on synthetic
shells. A book on furniture
refinishing will show you
techniques for repairing or
refinishing damaged wooden
drumshells.

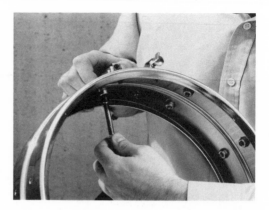

11. Measure the di-
mensions of the shell with a
ruler or tape measure.
Measure both depth and
diameter. You may find
that the drum is not the size

Close up of tension casing removal. Tension
casings are bolted to the shell from the inside.
(Courtesy of John Comber.)

you thought it was. Make note of the shell size so you will not have to guess
when you buy heads, cases or other parts.

12. Check the shell for roundness by measuring the diameter, starting
from several different points around the shell. Compare the measurements
and note any difference of more than 1/8″ or so. Repeat this at the other
end of the shell. Shells that are significantly out of round may be difficult
to tune. The more out of round, the greater the problem. If a new, top
quality drumhead of the correct size must be forced on or off the shell instead of fitting smoothly, there is definitely a problem. Modern shell construction methods usually produce shells with more precise dimensions
than were common in the 1960s or earlier (the difference in precision is
most notable in wooden shells). However, minor imprecision in shell
roundness causes fewer problems with tuning and sound quality than a
bearing edge that is not flat.

In rare instances, metal shells can be bent back into shape, but other
materials cannot. Badly out of round shells require replacement. Slightly
out of round shells are usable in most cases. Of course, if the shell is new
and significantly out of round, it should be replaced under warranty by the
manufacturer.

13. Wipe the bearing edges of the shell with a clean cloth. Check for
level bearing edges by placing the shell on a flat surface, bearing edge
down. Don't assume that your table or floor is perfectly flat. Usually a piece
of plate glass is flat enough for this test. If the shell obviously rocks back
and forth on the flat surface, the bearing edge is not level. A closer test is
whether you can slip the edge of a business card under the bearing edge
at any point. Alternately, you can put a light inside the drum and see if

Leveling the bearing edge of a wooden drumshell with sandpaper. *(Courtesy of John Comber.)*

it is visible at any point where the bearing edge meets the flat surface (tape a piece of paper to the glass for this test or use a flat surface that is not transparent). Remember that an uneven bearing edge can cause more tuning problems than a slightly out of round shell.

Not much can be done to fix an uneven bearing edge on a metal shell. Other materials can be filed and sanded to remove high spots. Drum repair professionals sometimes have power equipment that can cut a perfectly level edge with the desired angle and degree of sharpness. Doing it by hand is more time consuming.

Also remember that the resonator side of a snare drumshell has a snare bed cut into it, so it will not be level in those two areas. I advise you not to tamper with the snare bed, other than smooth-sanding of rough spots with very fine sandpaper. If it needs further attention, it is best left to an expert.

The simplest way to level a bearing edge by hand is by taping a large sheet of fine sandpaper to the flat surface you used to check for flatness. Place the shell on the sandpaper, bearing edge down. You can mark the high spots with pencil or ink to keep track of the area that needs to be worn down. Rotate the shell back and forth on the sandpaper using very little pressure. The object is to remove any high spots without wearing down the whole edge, so check the edge frequently as you work. At first, mainly the high spots will show wear. When sanding marks begin to show up on the lower areas, the bearing edge should be level. Measure it on the flat surface to check this. When the job is complete, repeat this procedure on the opposite end of the shell if a resonator head is used.

14. Run your finger around the edge to check for rough areas. There may be rough spots even if you did not sand the bearing edge. During the period when single headed drums were popular, many drummers removed the resonator heads from their bass drums and toms. The exposed bearing edges were often badly nicked and gouged during use and transport. If you plan to use resonator heads, these damaged areas must be smoothed. Small irregularities can be removed by the same procedure described for adjusting an uneven bearing edge.

15. The bearing edge should now be level and free of irregularities. It must be filed or sanded to restore the width and angle of edge desired. The high spots that received the most sanding will be wider than other areas. Without removing material from the very top of the edge, carefully file and or sand the inner and outer angles to make the contour consistent all around the shell. Finish with extremely fine sandpaper. Run your finger around the edge. It should feel smooth and even. Measure the edge again on the flat surface to check your work.

16. Clean the shell inside and out. Chromed metal shells may be cleaned with a good quality metal polish. Such polishes are available in liquid, paste and chemical-impregnated wadding form. Whenever possible, avoid abrasive polishes that might scratch the metal. Chemical-action polishes are safer, as long as they are designed for use on chrome. Rust and stubborn dirt can be removed with very fine grade steel wool, taking care not to rub too hard. To remove polish and or steel wool residue, chromed metal shells can be washed and immediately dried as described below.

Unchromed metal shells are usually coated with clear lacquer to prevent tarnish. Do not use polish or steel wool on these shells, as it will wear off the protective coating. Wash a lacquered metal shell with a soft sponge, warm water and liquid dishwashing detergent. Dry it immediately and thoroughly with a soft, clean cloth or towel.

Transparent acrylic shells and fiberglass shells can also be washed with a soft sponge, warm water and dishwashing liquid, then dried.

Wooden drumshells should not be immersed in water, as this might warp them. They can be wiped inside and out with a damp sponge and dried immediately. Alternatively, a mild cleaner or solvent that will not damage the interior or exterior finish can be used to wipe off any accumulated dirt. There are too many different types of interior and exterior finishes to be able to recommend a widely available, safe solvent for each one. If you are unsure of the suitability of such a cleaning product for your drums, you might first apply a small amount of it to an inconspicuous area of the shell and inspect for damage. When you have wiped down the shell, dry it completely before proceeding.

17. Repair any damage to the interior or exterior finish. Plastic wrap finishes that show signs of peeling away from the shell at the seams should be re-glued. Faded or mis-matched plastic wrap can be replaced. There are several companies that sell re-covering kits. Some of them advertise in the various drum magazines.

Wood grain or lacquer finishes with chips and scratches may be touched up. Badly pitted chrome plated metal shells may be re-chromed, but I would hesitate to trust a drumshell to most chrome plating shops. They are not used to handling musical instruments and the shell might come back beautifully plated, but out of round. Lacquered brass, copper or bronze shells can be stripped, polished and re-lacquered, if necessary, by a high quality repair shop that handles trumpets, saxophones or other brass musical instruments.

18. Before the drum is reassembled, wax the exterior finish. Waxing adds a protective layer that inhibits rust, tarnish and oxidation of paint. It also conceals minute scratches and makes the shell look shiny and new.

On painted finishes, rubbing the wax on and buffing it off removes a small amount of oxidized paint. This actually brightens the finish and does no harm. However, pearlescent paint often has metallic highlights in the color layer, sealed by clear lacquer. An abrasive wax may wear away the clear layer, damaging the finish. If you are not sure whether a particular brand of wax is suitable for the finish of your drums, follow the warnings on the label of the wax container. If that is inconclusive, try a small amount on an inconspicuous area of the shell and observe the result.

As a guideline, metal shells should be waxed inside and out for tarnish protection. Chrome plated shells can be waxed with any automotive wax that is safe for chrome. Lacquered metal shells require a gentle, non-abrasive wax like the spray waxes designed for wooden furniture. Plastic wrap finishes shine beautifully with most automotive waxes. Transparent acrylic shells can be waxed inside and out. If they are badly scratched, an abrasive, automotive wax may help to smooth out the minor scratches. Otherwise, use non-abrasive wax on acrylic. Wood grain finishes and pearlescent paints are best waxed with non-abrasive, spray furniture wax. Automotive wax works well on other painted finishes.

19. Coat the bearing edge(s) of the shell by rubbing with a block of paraffin wax. Every time you remove and replace a head on your drums,

the bearing edge should be wiped with a clean cloth and rubbed with paraffin wax. This lubricates the edge of the shell, creating a smooth surface for the underside of the head to slide across as it is being tensioned. Paraffin wax can be purchased at many grocery stores. It comes in blocks and is commonly used to seal glass containers when making jam or preserves.

20. The shell is now ready for reassembly. Cover it with a clean cloth to keep off dust and store it away from moisture and extreme temperatures until you are ready to install its hardware.

21. Disassemble any brackets, internal tone controls, snare strainers and butts, etc. Greasy parts, including the threads of bolts and screws can be cleaned in a bowl with isopropyl (rubbing) alcohol or any solvent that dissolves grease and is safe for the finish of the metal (usually chrome plating). An old toothbrush is a good tool for this type of cleaning. After drying the parts thoroughly, use any good quality chrome polish on all chrome plated parts that require further cleaning. My personal favorite is the chemical-impregnated wadding type, such as Nevr-Dull or Buckaroo cymbal cleaner. It will not scratch and it leaves very little residue. Follow this by waxing any chrome plated parts that do not have threads.

22. Apply a couple of drops of oil to any threaded parts except tension rods. This lubricates the threads to smooth the function and reduce wear. It also helps to prevent corrosion. Read the section on drumset hardware maintenance in this book for information on selecting the right oil. On snare drums, be sure to lubricate the moving parts of the snare strainer and throw-off mechanism. Store these parts in a clean parts tray. Make note of broken, worn or missing parts and purchase replacements.

23. Disassemble tension casings containing springs. Remove the springs and threaded inserts. Note whether there is any resonance deadening material behind the springs. Clean and polish the empty tension casings, then wax them. If much dirt has found its way into the casings, the springs will have to be wiped clean.

24. Clean and polish the outside of the threaded inserts. Quite a bit of dirt can collect on them, preventing them from flexing properly to align with the tension rods. Clean the internal threads of the inserts with cotton swabs dipped in rubbing alcohol. Cotton swabs can be purchased in the baby-care section of most pharmacies. Threading a cotton swab through an insert as though you are screwing in a tension rod removes any dirt and old oil or grease. This step is very important to facilitate smooth, precise tuning. Threading a second, dry swab through the insert will remove most of the rubbing alcohol and more dirt. Allow the inserts to dry thoroughly before reassembling (the remaining rubbing alcohol will evaporate and leave no noticeable residue). Test each one by screwing in a clean tension rod and replace any inserts that have stripped internal threads.

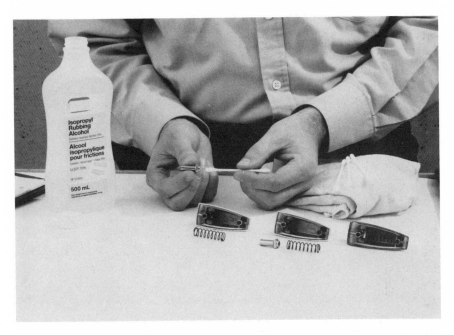

Tension casings with springs and threaded inserts assembled and disassembled. Rubbing alcohol and swab are used to clean inside threaded insert. *(Courtesy of John Comber.)*

25. Often the springs inside the tension casings resonate when the drum is struck. In many situations, this noise is not loud enough to be a problem but in recording studios or during live performances where microphones are used on the drums, it may be objectionable. In any case, this problem is easy to eliminate. Some manufacturers stuff a piece of felt or foam rubber behind the spring in the tension casing. This muffles the resonance of the spring. If your tension casings lack this feature, purchase a package of absorbent puffs (also called cotton balls or cosmetic puffs) at a pharmacy. Place one or more of these puffs in each tension casing before installing the threaded insert and spring. In most cases, this will dampen the spring vibration and cure the problem. If you wish to take no chances, you can replace the springs with pieces of clear plastic tubing. This is sold as fuel line in automotive parts stores or as aquarium hose in pet shops. Select tubing with the correct inside diameter to fit the end of the threaded insert. Cut it in lengths sufficient to hold the insert in place and use it instead of the spring. The tubing is flexible enough to allow the insert to flex and align itself with the tension rod, but it will not resonate like a spring.

26. When you have reassembled the threaded insert and spring (or

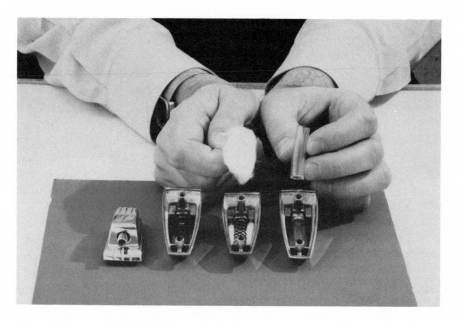

Threaded inserts reassembled, showing, left to right, exterior view; interior view with no spring damping; interior view with cotton ball to muffle spring vibrations; interior view with plastic tubing replacing spring. *(Courtesy of John Comber.)*

tubing) in the tension casing, put a drop of oil on the screws that hold the tension casings to the shell. Place all these parts in a clean parts tray, note any broken, worn or missing bits and purchase replacements.

27. Some manufacturers use thin rubber, plastic or felt gaskets between the shell and the tension casings. They minimize damage to the exterior finish of the shell when the tension casing is tightened in place and help to isolate the casing acoustically from the shell. If you wish to fit similar gaskets on your drums, purchase a sheet of thin, felt cloth. Cut your own gaskets, using the tension casings to trace the correct size onto the felt. You will have to punch holes for the mounting screws to pass through the felt gaskets.

28. Check the counterhoops for warpage. They should sit without wobbling on a flat surface. If not, it may be difficult to tune the drum precisely. Measure their diameter at several points for roundness. Slight variations in profile or roundness are acceptable. Sometimes out of round pressed steel counterhoops can be bent back into shape. Any hoop that is so warped or out of round that it will not fit without binding or interference on a new, top quality drumhead of the correct size should be replaced.

29. Clean and polish the counterhoops, then wax them. Good quality

chrome polish will remove most dirt and tarnish. Fine grade steel wool can be used to remove any stubborn rust. Rub gently, so as not to damage the chrome plating. Remember to clean the often neglected underside of the counterhoops. Place them in a clean parts tray.

Wooden bass drum counterhoops require different treatment. Start by cleaning them with solvent. Their finish often becomes chipped. A few chips or scratches can be touched up with a small brush and paint or varnish, depending on their finish. When they are completely dry, waxing finishes the job. All-around rough appearance requires complete sanding and repainting or varnishing. If the whole counterhoop requires refinishing, it is usually easier to obtain a smooth finish with spray paints rather than brush painting. If the counterhoop has an inlay of plastic drumshell finish, carefully peel it off before sanding and glue it back in place (contact cement usually works well in this application) when the paint has dried.

30. Clean the threads of the tension rods with an old toothbrush and rubbing alcohol or other solvent. Dry them thoroughly. Clean the tension rod washers with solvent and dry them. Place them all in a clean parts tray.

31. Inspect each tension rod carefully. Replace any that are corroded, bent, stripped or of improper length or thread size. Replace missing or worn out tension rod washers. When purchasing new tension rods, order the exact part you need from the drum manufacturer's parts catalog or bring a sample with you to the music store for comparison purposes. It is a good idea to keep a few spare tension rods and washers handy for each drum in case of emergencies.

32. Apply a thin coating of grease to the threads of the tension rods. This lubricates the threads, reduces wear and prevents corrosion. A small dab of grease under the head of the rod where it contacts the washer is also a good idea. Lubricating tension rods properly is important to assure smooth, precise tuning. Grease is preferable to oil in this application because it is less likely to run off and it provides smoother tuning under high tension.

Of the various types of grease I have tried over the years, the best results have been achieved with silicone greases, such as Dow Corning #44 grease. Some greases (petroleum jelly for example) attract dust. This acts like sandpaper on the threads of the tuning hardware, increasing wear and preventing smooth tuning. That means more frequent cleaning and reapplication of grease. Silicone grease tends to be anti-static, so it will not attract dust as readily. Grease containing molybdenum disulphide reduces the co-efficient of friction between metal parts too much, causing some people to over-tighten fittings. It also leaves black stains on anything it touches. Silicone grease does not create these problems. Some greases are mineral oil thickened with a lithium soap. Exposure to the air eventually makes them gummy, which necessitates frequent cleaning and reapplication. The Dow Corning #44 is a silicone fluid in a lithium soap thickener that withstands long exposure to air without deteriorating. It is available at many bearing supply or industrial supply companies.

33. If the heads you removed from the drum are unsuitable, broken or worn out, purchase new ones. If they are used but still in good condition, clean them before reinstalling them. Head selection, cleaning, etc. are described in the drumhead section of this book.

34. Place a clean cloth on your work table. Put the previously cleaned drumshell on the cloth. Install the tension casings on the shell. Do not overtighten their mounting screws, but do not leave them loose, either. A firm, but gentle hand on the screwdriver will prevent stripped threads.

35. Install mounting brackets, internal tone controls and similar hardware. On snare drums, install the snare strainer and butt. Again, tighten firmly without overtightening. If you have forgotten the exact location of these items on the shell, matching the item with the mounting holes on the shell should help make it clear.

36. Before you install the heads, find the location of the drum's serial number. On some drums, it is stamped on the manufacturer's name plate on the exterior of the shell. On others, it is on a paper label glued to the inside of the shell. Record this number. It can help police to identify and recover the drum if it is stolen. It may also be required if you insure your drumset against theft or damage.

37. Position the shell batter side up and place the batter head on the drumshell. I like to align the trademark on the drumhead with the trademark on the drumshell. By making this a habit, I never have to remember the position of the head when I remove it. Drumheads seat themselves to the shell in the position in which they are installed. Reinstalling them in the same position makes them easier to get back in tune.

38. Place the counterhoop over the head and align the holes in the counterhoop with the tension casings on the shell.

39. Insert the tension rods through the holes in the counterhoop with a washer under the head of each rod. Set each tension rod onto the threaded insert beneath it.

40. Using your fingers or your drum tuning key, thread each tension rod into its threaded insert until the head of each tension rod rests against the counterhoop (with a washer separating them from direct contact).

41. Seat the head and tune it. This is described in the tuning section of this book. If the drum uses a resonator head, turn the drum resonator side up and repeat from step 37 above to install it.

42. For snare drums, wipe the snare strands carefully with a clean cloth

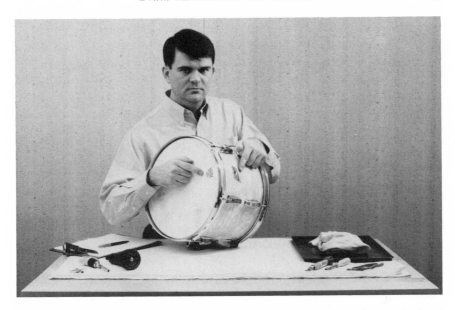

Install heads with trademark lined up to drumshell trademark, making it easy to remove and refit the head in the same position. *(Courtesy of John Comber.)*

to remove dust or dirt (if the snares are particularly dirty, wipe them carefully with solvent). Set the coiled wire snares on a flat surface and examine them. If the snare unit twists instead of lying flat, replace it with new snares. If there are broken or badly bent strands, use wire cutters to snip them off as close as possible to the end plates. Do not leave sharp points that could puncture the snare head. File them off if necessary. If several strands are broken off or bent, purchase new snares. Coiled wire snares eventually lose their resilience due to constant stretching. Usually they will require replacement due to damage before the metal is stretched out. Snapped strands are often an indication of metal fatigue.

43. If the snares use cord, tape or plastic strips to attach them to the strainer and butt, examine this material. Cord eventually frays and breaks, usually at the point where it passes through the holes in the snare end plates. Inspect this area frequently and replace the cord when it shows signs of wear. Appropriate cord is available from several drum and accessory companies. It lasts longer and works much better than string, twine or other inappropriate substitutes. Keep some spare cord with you. In an emergency, try using a pair of thin, nylon shoe laces as a short term substitute. It is best to replace them with the proper cord at your earliest opportunity. Joe Montineri (who manufactures custom snare drums) sells a heavy duty "super" snare cord that may be useful if you tend to break cord frequently.

Tape is usually of the fabric-reinforced variety. It eventually wears and spare material should be kept on hand. Plastic strips also wear out at the point where they pass through the slot in the snare end plate. Spares can be made inexpensively by cutting narrow strips from a worn out plastic drumhead. The main problem to watch for with both tape and plastic strips is their tendency to slip out of the clamping mechanisms at the strainer and butt when the snares are tensioned. You can minimize this by roughening the material slightly with sandpaper to give it more grip. Another trick is to run the ends of the tape or plastic to the top of the clamping mechanism, bend them over and clamp them. This 180 degree bend is less likely to pull out than feeding the plastic or tape directly into the clamping mechanism from the bottom.

44. Place the snares on the snare head and position them so that the ends are equidistant from the counterhoop. Secure the cord, tape or plastic strips to the strainer and butt.

45. Tension the snares. This is described in the tuning section of this book.

Your drums should now be looking, functioning and sounding their best. Regular attention will keep them that way.

Choosing the Right Drums

When I started playing drums in 1964, it was relatively easy to choose the right equipment. The vast majority of drumsets for all styles of popular music consisted of a 14" × 22" bass drum, a 5" × 14" snare drum, a 9" × 13" mounted tom and a 16" × 16" floor tom. Not as much was known about the variables that affect drum sound. The biggest choice most of us had to make was between a wood shell or metal shell snare drum. If you had a drumset like this from any of the better quality manufacturers, you were well equipped.

Drummers now have more choices. The basic, entry-level drumset has expanded to five drums. Shells are often extended depth sizes. There is more emphasis on selecting components for specific applications. Making the right decision can be a confusing process.

Drumsets are often described by the number of "pieces" they contain. Since not everyone is familiar with this terminology, it should be understood that a piece in this context refers to a drum. For example, a five-piece drumset consists of five drums, the related pedals and stands (known as hardware) and the cymbals. No matter how many extra stands, cymbals, cases, cow bells or other miscellaneous bits of percussion equipment are included, a set with five drums is a five-piece drumset. When describing any drumset, the number of drums is the number of pieces.

You may be facing the purchase of your first drumset, thinking about your next set or just evaluating your current equipment. There are a few considerations that could make your choice easier.

The first is cost. A drumset is a substantial investment. If money is no object, you can choose from the best quality new equipment available, buying as many drums as you want. If, like most of us, your budget will not stretch that far, you will limit yourself to a smaller or less expensive new set or a good quality used drumset.

Become familiar with what is available and how much it costs by visiting your local music shops, reading the ads in drum magazines, checking the classified ads in your local newspaper and writing to manufacturers for catalogs and price lists. If you are just starting, remember that your budget must cover the cost of drums, cymbals, hardware, cases, drumsticks, etc.

New equipment is usually covered by a manufacturer's warranty. Reputable music stores sometimes offer a limited warranty on used equipment. Privately purchased used equipment has no warranty and should be examined very carefully before buying. Take a good look at new drumsets, too. Don't worry about a few stick marks on the heads. You must expect those if you are allowed to try the drums before buying, as you should. However, shipping damage or nicks and scratches received on the showroom floor are best discussed before you take the set home.

If you are thinking of buying a basic, new drumset and adding to it at a later date, stick with brand names of known quality and reputation. Also, stick to one of the more popular finishes, such as black, white or red. By doing this, there is more chance that additional, matching equipment will still be available when you come back to buy a couple of extra toms or a second bass drum. Some manufacturers make frequent changes in their product lines and there are frequent additions and deletions to some manufacturers' lists of drumshell finishes.

Many manufacturers offer both professional quality and budget priced drumsets. This is also true for the manufacturers of cymbals, hardware and other equipment. Do some research by reading catalogs so you will know the difference. There is nothing wrong with buying the less expensive items, but inexperienced drummers may think they are getting a bargain on top quality equipment when they are really paying full price for less expensive merchandise with the same brand name. If you are not familiar with a company's product line, it is particularly easy to be fooled this way when buying used equipment. Know what you are buying.

Significant savings can be had by purchasing used drums. If you need top quality equipment, you can often buy it used for the same cost as a new set of lesser quality. But condition is a big factor. Do not make the mistake of buying a beaten up used set with missing and broken parts, thinking you can fix it up cheaply. Parts can be quite expensive. The price of abused or incomplete drumsets must reflect the cost of fixing them up. For the same reason, you should avoid obsolete used drums unless you know a good source of spare parts for them.

When considering a used drumset, ask to see the current owner's bill of sale. You want to be sure that the drums are not stolen or still partially owned by a finance company. When you buy used drums, have the owner write a bill of sale for you so that you will have proof of ownership. Careful reading of the information in this book will show you the common areas of breakage and other problems on drum equipment. Use this knowledge when examining used equipment.

When deciding whether to trade in your current drumset or sell it privately, you should know that a retail music store can only afford to give you "wholesale" value for it. Just like a car dealer accepting a trade-in, the music store must replace parts and fix anything wrong before marking up the price and trying to sell the equipment at a profit for their time, trouble and expense. You may be able to get more for your drumset by selling it privately, but you will have to absorb the expense of putting the set in good shape and advertising it. Then you may spend a lot of time answering calls and showing it to potential buyers without receiving an adequate offer. It is worth weighing these alternatives when the time comes to change drumsets.

Your drumset must suit your needs as well as your budget. Are you a novice drummer, a full time professional or somewhere in between? Do you play along with records at home, play with a school ensemble, play dances or parties on weekends or tour with a full time traveling band? The answers to these questions indicate the minimum quality of equipment you require to give good service.

Often, the difference between professional quality drums and more moderately priced drums has as much to do with durability as sound quality. Adequate sound can be obtained from inexpensive drums but they may not last as long as professional equipment because they do not have the same quality of materials and construction. The amount of use, especially involving moving, setting up and dismantling is the determining factor.

The true cost of drum equipment for comparison purposes is measured by its initial cost spread over its life expectancy. Then add the expected cost of maintenance during this service life and subtract the expected re-sale value. Full or part time professionals should buy the best quality drumset they can afford. Take care of it and it will cost you less in the long run than cheaper equipment, while doing a better job and maintaining a higher resale value. Novices or hobby drummers do not usually subject their drumsets to as much wear and tear. Moderately priced equipment from a quality manufacturer will last them for many years with reasonable care.

The number of drums you need and their individual sizes should be determined by your level of experience, the styles of music you play, the places you perform and your method of moving the equipment.

The first time drumset buyer should purchase a complete, matching, basic drumset. When buying new drums, it is often cheaper to get the whole set at once as opposed to buying one or two drums at a time. This also insures that all the drums will match. Mismatched equipment has a lower resale value for purely cosmetic reasons, although variations such as chrome plated snare drums with otherwise matching-finish sets are traditionally acceptable and can be seen in many drum catalogs. A four- or five-piece drumset straight from the catalog of a quality manufacturer will have a compatible range of drum sizes. You can handle almost any style of popular music with this amount of equipment.

The experienced drummer may have more specific requirements and preferences. Most of us fantasize at one time or another about playing elaborate, double bass drumsets with eight or nine toms. A few years experience teaches us that being a good drummer has nothing to do with the number of drums in our set. Large drumsets do allow us to explore new musical ideas and develop our technique in different ways. There are some styles of music where large numbers of drums and large drum sizes are fashionable and sometimes necessary. They certainly look impressive and visual appeal is an important part of some musical styles.

But big drumsets have their disadvantages. Too much equipment cannot be utilized properly until some basic skills are developed. For any drummer who moves his or her own equipment, large drums and or large numbers of drums can be difficult to fit on a small stage or in a small car. They are heavier and bulkier to carry and take longer to set up than a basic set. Also, the more drums in your set, the more it costs. The professional whose budget is limited should buy a smaller number of top quality drums rather than a large number of inexpensive drums.

Sheer volume is not a factor in selecting drum size. If a drum's volume was determined primarily by its size, bass drums would be much louder than snare drums and smaller toms, which is not necessarily the case. The difference of a few inches in drumshell size affects pitch and tonal quality, but not volume to any significant degree. If you know how to select the appropriate drumhead and how to tune it, almost any size drum produces adequate volume for musical styles requiring no amplification.

Microphones or other pickup devices have become almost mandatory for the acoustic drumset in rock band performances. Shure Brothers, a microphone manufacturer, publishes a booklet called "Microphone Techniques for Music" containing a section that shows recommended microphone placement on the acoustic drumset and microphone choice for each component of the drumset. The Beyer microphone company has a chart with similar information.

Both pitch and tonal quality are related in part to drum size. The larger diameter, deeper shells favored by rock drummers contribute to the low-pitched sounds they often prefer. Beyond a certain point, however, increased shell size can have a negative effect on tonal quality that must be compensated for by head selection and careful tuning. Bass drumshells larger than 24" diameter begin to sound very boomy, without clear definition of each stroke. Toms of 18" or greater diameter may experience the same problem. This is one of the practical reasons for the introduction of extended shell depths. The so-called "power" shell depths alter pitch and tonal quality rather than volume. By extending the depth of a 22" or 24" diameter bass drumshell from 14" to 16", you lower the pitch slightly and emphasize the lower frequencies that the drum produces. This often produces better results than the use of a 26" or larger diameter bass drum. The same holds true for toms, where the smaller head diameters give better definition to each stroke, while deeper shells lower the pitch. For those who like low pitched drums, the deeper shell allows you to use a smaller diameter drum (and more tension on the head for good stick response) while maintaining the low pitch. Increasing depth has its point of diminishing returns, though. Bass drums with shells deeper than 16" and toms with "square" dimensions such as 12" × 12" or 13" × 13" must be tuned carefully to avoid loss of definition. This has always been obvious on the standard floor tom size of 16" × 16".

Smaller diameter, shallower drumshell sizes contribute to higher pitch and better definition of each stroke. The smaller the shell, the shorter the sustain and the less boomy the sound. If you like this tonal quality, stick to shells in smaller sizes and conventional depths. If you prefer this tonal quality but like somewhat lower pitch, the use of smaller than usual shell diameters with extended shell depths can be the answer. For instance, a 16" × 20" bass drum, 9" × 10", 11" × 12" and 14" × 14" toms as opposed to 22", 12", 14" and 16" diameter drums respectively. The 14" floor tom will sacrifice a bit of low pitch potential compared to the 16", but will have better definition.

Snare drum sizes vary primarily in depth, most being of 14" diameter.

The most versatile is probably the 6½" depth, which can be tuned high for a crisp sound or tuned low for a deeper, punchy sound. If you want deep pitch while retaining high tension for good stick response, depths of 8" or even 10" should be considered. If you prefer a higher pitched, brighter sound, 5" depth or even the 3" depth piccolo snare drums are a good choice, although the piccolo, like the 10" deep snare drum, is not as versatile. If your work covers a variety of musical styles, you may decide to purchase different snare drums for different applications.

Single headed bass drums and toms produce a more definite fundamental pitch with fewer overtones and less sustain than double headed drums. Their attack seems louder because there is no resonator head to diffuse it. They are also more difficult to play because no air is compressed inside the shell when you strike the head, producing less stick response.

Although there may be times when you want this single headed sound, you should generally avoid buying drums with no provision for resonator heads. A single headed drum can produce only this sound, while a double headed drum is more versatile. If you want the sound of concert toms and a single headed bass drum, you can get it by cutting away part of the resonator head, as is common on bass drums, or by removing the resonator head temporarily.

When you are considering different shell materials, interior finishes, bearing edge configurations and other variables, you should use side by side comparison tests whenever possible. Remember that the type of head and the way the head is tuned and muffled will create a more noticeable difference in most cases than will these other factors. You would have to compare drums with identical heads and tuning to isolate the factors that you are listening for. The most obvious difference will be between metal shell and wood shell snare drums, that same choice that drummers have faced for years.

Let your ears be your guide, rather than basing your decision solely on technical information. Have someone else play the drums while you listen from a distance to hear what the audience will hear. The more drums you try, the more you will find yourself drawn to certain types, sizes and brands. You will begin to define "your" drum sound. Any drumset you own that does not give you that sound will be unsatisfactory, regardless of how expensive or elaborate it is.

Drumheads

The drumhead is the part of the drum that you strike to produce the sound. It is a membrane stretched across the end of the shell cylinder. More than any other feature of material or construction, the drumhead is the greatest contributing factor to the sound of the drum.

Materials and Construction

Drumheads were originally made of calfskin. Some drummers still refer to heads as "skins." The simplest, non-tunable drumhead consists of a piece of calfskin tacked directly to the drumshell. Traditional, tunable calfskin heads consist of a piece of calfskin wrapped and tucked around a wooden or metal hoop. The hoop fits over the diameter of the shell and is pulled down by the tuning hardware. This tightens the calfskin across the end of the shell.

Calfskin heads are still used on some bongo and conga drums but they are now far less common on drumsets. Being a natural material, calfskin is affected by changes in humidity. In dry weather, it can split as it dries and tightens. In wet weather, it becomes loose and soggy. Calfskin heads require careful maintenance and frequent tuning. Sonor is one of the few companies still producing some calfskin heads for drumset use.

The introduction of the plastic drumhead in the 1950s solved these problems. Most plastic heads are made of Mylar, which is not affected by humidity. Mylar is generally stronger than calfskin and will take a great deal of punishment, but it may be brittle at low temperatures and should be treated carefully when cold.

Other synthetic material heads are made from woven fabric, usually combined with plastic resins or laminated to a layer of Mylar. Examples of this type of head construction are the Remo Falams K series or the heads from Cana-Sonic or Compo.

Plastic heads consist of sheets of plastic permanently attached to metal or plastic hoops. The plastic is secured by filling the hoop with an epoxy-type glue to hold it in place or by clamping the plastic

Remo Powerstroke heads have a rubber ring on the hoop designed to prevent the head from pulling out from under the drum's batter counterhoop during high tension use. *(Courtesy of Remo, Inc.)*

between the component pieces of metal that form the hoop. Remo and Evans are examples of companies that use primarily glued head construction, while Aquarian, Ludwig, Premier and Sonor are examples of companies that use some form of clamped head construction.

Plastic hoops are sometimes useful for their ability to conform to an out-of-round drumshell or uneven bearing edge. These problems are less common on modern, professional quality drumshells than on older drums, due to the different shell construction methods and more precise manufacturing tolerances now used by most companies. Among metal hoops, some will be found to be quite firm, while others are more flexible. A hoop that deforms under tension makes precise tuning more difficult, while a more rigid hoop facilitates even tuning.

There is a minor variance in shell diameters of the same nominal size between different drum manufacturers. This is sometimes due to the difference between a bearing edge formed at the outside edge of the shell or beveled slightly toward the inside. Heads of the same nominal size may also vary slightly between manufacturers. This is usually not enough to prevent the head from fitting the shell, but it can prevent the bearing edge of the shell from meeting the head at the exact spot where the curve of the collar begins. During manufacture, the plastic is molded to fit over a drumshell so that the hoop is slightly below the level of the playing surface. The distance between the playing surface and the hoop is called the collar of the head. Some heads have deep collars while others have shallow collars. If the head has a sharply defined "corner" where the collar begins, a less than exact fit will cause wrinkles in the head and undesirable overtones at low tension.

Remo Pinstripe heads are an example of two-ply construction with the plies glued together at the perimeter. *(Courtesy of Remo, Inc.)*

The traditional method for solving this problem is to seat the head on the shell. The procedure is explained in the section on drum tuning and muffling in this book. It is necessary to stretch the head to re-form this sharp corner, making it conform to the contour and diameter of the bearing edge. Aquarian drumheads avoid this problem by using a gradual curve instead of a sharp corner at the collar.

A calfskin head is mounted on a drum while wet and then lightly tensioned, creating a collar. As it dries, it retains this shape. Changes in humidity and the stress of playing the head cause it to stretch. Retensioning deepens the collar until, in extreme cases, the tensioning mechanisms reach the limit of their adjustment. At this point, a traditionally constructed calfskin head can be removed, moistened and re-tucked on its hoop to take up the slack.

Any plastic or other permanently constructed head that is badly stretched must be replaced. Re-tucking is impossible due to the nature of the plastic material and its permanent attachment to the hoop. In general, drumheads have a limited service life. They are subject to more wear than any other part of the drum. You should expect to replace your drumheads when they break or wear out or when their sound deteriorates.

Head Breakage and Wear

The most common methods of head breakage are punctures, splits or tears and pulling out of the hoop. Punctures are often caused by sharp pieces of drum hardware during set-up or transport. Handling the drums carefully and packing them in cases will minimize this problem. Heads often split or tear due to heavy or improper playing. Selecting the correct head and stick for the application and striking the drum properly will minimize this type of breakage. High tension puts a lot of stress on the area where the head material is attached to the hoop. Selecting the correct head for extreme tension applications will help prevent pull-out. However, if any

Remo Ebony series heads are an example of colored plastic for cosmetic reasons available in several functional variations. *(Courtesy of Remo, Inc.)*

new head pulls out under normal tension while being installed, it is defective.

If you select the correct heads for the application and take reasonable care of them, you may never break a head. The amount of time it takes for a head to wear out depends on your playing style, how often you play, how you tension your heads and whether you need optimal sound quality from your drums.

More use equals more wear, so your heads may last for years if you do not use your drumset frequently. Hard use also accelerates wear, so the heavy, loud drummer will need new heads sooner than the light player. Highly tensioned heads do not dent as readily or deeply as heads that are loosely tensioned. The drummer in a recording studio will be more concerned with precise tuning and optimal sound quality than most novices or hobby drummers. If you are fussy about the sound of your drums, you will replace heads when their sound begins to deteriorate even if they are not otherwise worn out. Decreased stick response (less bounce) even after re-tensioning is a good indicator of a head needing replacement. Writing the date of installation near the edge of a new head with a felt tip pen (never a hard point pen, which might puncture the head) is a simple way of keeping track of the age and service life of your drumheads.

Selecting Your Drumheads

Plastic (or other synthetic material) drumheads are currently supplied as original equipment by all major drum manufacturers. When they were first introduced, they were not universally accepted, due to the difference in tonal quality between calfskin and plastic. The wide variety of plastic heads now available offers drummers many different sound and appearance options. Picking the correct head for the application requires careful consideration.

The first thing to consider is correct size. Drumheads designed for drumset use are made in a range of sizes from 6" to 40" diameter, in one or two inch increments. You should know the size of head required for each of your drums to save guesswork when the time comes to buy replacements. Heads are sized according to the diameter of the drumshell that they fit. When you ask for a 14" head at your local music store, it is assumed that you are actually asking for a head to fit a 14" diameter drumshell. The head itself is larger than 14" from edge to edge in order to fit over the shell. This example holds true for any size of head. To determine drumshell size, you must remove the head and measure the outside diameter of the shell.

Although modern drums from quality manufacturers take standard inch-size heads, you may encounter older drums with non-standard shell diameters. These are usually metric-sized shells that fall between the more common inch equivalents. Although it is sometimes possible to order heads to fit these drums or have them specially made, you should avoid the extra time, trouble and expense by sticking to standard sizes.

The next consideration is quality. There are several reputable companies making professional quality drumheads. Choose from their product line based on your personal preferences and you can be reasonably sure of getting a durable, well made product. When experimenting with heads of unknown quality, you should try one before buying enough to fit all your drums. If it lives up to your expectations, you can buy more. If not, you have avoided a substantial waste of money. The same advice holds true when trying a different type of head from a well known manufacturer.

Quality will not be the concern, but you will be experimenting with different tonal characteristics. There are so many variables involved that it is difficult to predict exactly how a certain type of head will sound on your drums.

The next consideration is function. All drumheads are used in one of two ways. Batter heads are the heads that are struck when playing the drums. Resonator heads are fitted to the other end of the shell, opposite the batter head. Obviously all drums have batter heads, but some drums use no resonator heads or only partial resonator heads. The function of the batter head is to produce the desired sound while withstanding the stress of playing. Resonator heads are not struck, so they do not have to be as strong. They contribute to the sound of the drum by vibrating or resonating when you strike the batter head. All types of heads other than snare heads may be used for either batter or resonator function, although some are more suitable for one application than the other. Many drummers use different combinations of batter and resonator heads for different types of music or different volume levels.

"Snare head" is the term used to denote the special resonator head of a snare drum. Snare heads are the thinnest heads available. Usually transparent, they are far too thin to withstand striking and are used only in this one application. The special function of the snare head is to transmit the vibration of each stroke on the batter head to the snares. Any other type of head used for this function would be too thick to transmit these vibrations effectively.

Many drummers neglect to replace their resonator heads and snare heads periodically, thinking that they can not be worn out because they are not played. While they do not wear out as frequently as batter heads, their tonal quality does eventually deteriorate due to tensioning. Try fitting new ones and notice the improvement in sound quality.

Another variable to consider is the appearance of a drumhead. This can be confusing, because the difference between some heads is purely cosmetic, while the appearance of others is related to their tonal properties. There is nothing wrong with choosing a visually interesting head as long as its functional characteristics are compatible with its intended application. The best way to assess this is to read any literature published by the head manufacturer. I hesitate to make generalizations, as they might be misleading. For instance, the difference between different colored heads is purely cosmetic with some manufacturers and functionally related in other cases.

Disregarding functional differences for the moment, there are many appearance options. Examples of this are the colored heads offered by many manufacturers in either smooth or textured finish, including the traditional white. There are heads with center dots in black, white, silver and several other colors. Reflective "mirror" heads in chrome and gold are also available. Transparent heads and coatings imitating the look of calf-skin are other possibilities. Indications are that this variety will continue to increase.

One generalization about head appearance that is valid concerns surface texture. A smooth, plastic batter head on the snare drum provides poor brush response. Drummers who use brushes require a snare drum batter head with a textured surface to create the necessary "swish" sound as the brushes are swept across the head. Coated heads from most manufacturers work well in this application when new. The rough surface coating eventually wears off, necessitating head replacement to maintain sound quality. Remo's Fiberskyn 2 heads produce good brush sound, but wire brushes sometimes catch and tear their coating. Many of the fabric heads, such as Compo and Cana-Sonic, are constructed from woven fabric with an integral textured surface that is good for brush work and does not wear off.

The next thing to consider is head thickness, which affects sensitivity, durability and tonal quality. The thickness of a head and its resulting characteristics are determined in three ways. First, it is determined by the thickness of each plastic ply (or other material) used to construct the playing surface. Second, by the number of full or partial plies in its construction. Third, by any coating applied to the playing surface, between the plies or to the underside of the head. The terms thickness and weight are often used interchangeably when discussing drumheads.

The degree of sensitivity is important for both batter and resonator heads. The thinner the head, the less mass it has and the easier it vibrates. The thicker the head, the more mass it has and the more energy is needed to make it vibrate. Drummers who play at very low volume and frequently use brushes sometimes prefer the extra sensitivity of thin batter heads. Heavy players produce much more volume and do not require this degree of sensitivity from a batter head.

The resonator head is not stimulated directly, but responds to the vibration of the batter head. This vibration travels through the air column inside the shell and (to a lesser extent) through the shell material. If you have ever mistakenly fitted a batter head on the resonator side of a snare drum, you will understand why snare heads are so thin. A thicker head soaks up too much of the vibration before transmitting it to the snares.

Some manufacturers offer different thicknesses of snare heads to produce the desired degree of sensitivity. Medium weight snare heads are suitable for all-around playing. Lightweight snare heads are more sensitive and a better choice for low volume playing, while heavyweight snare heads are used most often in marching bands or occasionally by heavy rock drummers for reasons of durability. Most snare heads are transparent, single-ply material with no coating or reinforcement. An exception is the Hi-Performance snare head from Aquarian. It features sections of reinforcing material laminated to its underside at the two spots where the ends of a coiled wire snare unit contact the head. This allows the use of a regular thickness snare head for sensitivity, while minimizing the danger of snare wire punctures during heavy use.

The resonator head of a tom or bass drum contributes just as much to the drum's sensitivity, but this is not as evident because toms and bass drums do not have snares. The less mass/thickness in a resonator head, the more sensitive the drum. The more mass/thickness, the less sensitive the drum. It is important to consider the sensitivity of resonator heads in conjunction with the tonal characteristics affected by head thickness.

Durability in a drumhead refers to its ability to withstand wear and breakage. Durability is more important for batter heads than resonator heads, as previously mentioned. The most durable heads currently available are probably those made from woven synthetic fibers such as Kevlar in conjunction with Mylar or plastic resins. Kevlar is used in bulletproof vests for its puncture resistant properties. Examples of this type of head are the Remo Falams K series or the Compo Attack series.

More conventional plastic heads use greater ply thickness, two-ply construction or partial reinforcement of the playing surface to increase durability. The thickness of a layer of plastic is usually expressed in mils (thousandths of an inch). Single-ply heads from some manufacturers are all the same thickness, while others offer options in ply thickness among otherwise identical heads. Two-ply construction refers to heads with two full plies of plastic from edge to edge. Two thick plies offer greater strength than two thin plies. Examples of two-ply construction include Remo Emperor and Pinstripe heads, Evans Rock heads and Sonor XP heads.

The most common method of reinforcing a single-ply head is the center "dot," which is a layer of material laminated to the playing surface. Self-adhesive, plastic dots can be purchased and applied to any head with a smooth surface, but several manufacturers offer these heads ready made. Examples are Remo Sound Control heads, Ludwig Silver Dot heads, Sonor Controlled Power heads and Aquarian Power Dot heads. In most cases, the center dot is made from the same plastic material as the head. Aquarian uses a plastic impregnated fiber composite dot on their Mylar heads for greater flexibility.

Aquarian Hi-Performance heads have a unique method of reinforcement. A continuous, plastic spiral is laminated to the underside of the head. In addition to increasing durability, the spiral prevents a tear in the head from developing into a long split if the drummer must continue playing when the head breaks.

Snare drum and bass drum batter heads are struck more frequently than tom batter heads, making them the first to break or wear out in most musical situations. For this reason, some of the special purpose heads developed for extra durability are available only in snare drum (and sometimes bass drum) sizes. If you are not a particularly heavy player, you may not need the durability of thicker heads. However, you may choose them in some applications for their tonal characteristics.

The tonal quality of a drumhead, expressed in a simplified manner, is the way in which it emphasizes fundamental pitch or overtones. Fundamental pitch is the basic note produced at a particular level of tension, while overtones include the high pitched, ringy portion of the sound. Tuning and muffling techniques can modify this, but each type of head has a characteristic, potential ratio of fundamental pitch to overtones. Heads with a substantial amount of overtone are described as sounding bright or resonant, while heads with less overtone are described as sounding warm or mellow.

In general, heads with the least mass/thickness are the brightest sounding, while those with the greatest mass/thickness are the warmest sounding. Here are some of the more common head types in approximate order from brightest to most mellow:

    single-ply (transparent or colored) uncoated
    single-ply coated
    single-ply uncoated with center dot
    single-ply coated with center dot
    two-ply (transparent or colored) uncoated
    two-ply coated
    two-ply uncoated with glue between plies at perimeter
    two-ply coated with glue between plies at perimeter
    woven fabric composite heads
    two-ply uncoated with oil between plies

Not all variations of heads are covered in this list. You may find heads with tonal characteristics that do not seem to fit where they have been placed on the list. Slight design differences between manufacturers provide drummers with many choices and apparently similar heads from different companies may differ noticeably in sound.

Some design variations have not been mentioned elsewhere. For instance, an example of a two-ply head with oil between the plies is the Evans Hydraulic. Examples of two-ply heads with the plies glued together at the perimeter are Remo Pinstripe and Sonor XP series. Some manufacturers avoid the decreased sensitivity of a two-ply head and still achieve a significant reduction of overtones by other methods. For example, Aquarian Studio X heads are single-ply with an acoustic muffling ring laminated to their underside.

The presence or absence of a significant amount of overtone will tend to alter your perception of a head's pitch. Thin, bright sounding heads will seem to be higher pitched than thick, mellow sounding heads. Thin heads may also seem louder, as the high pitched, ringy portion of the sound gives a head crisp attack and projects or "cuts" better than a deeper, warmer sounding thick head. Beyond a certain point, increasing the mass of a drumhead does decrease its volume along with its overtones. In loud volume situations where the drums are not amplified, some of this ring is necessary if the drums are to be heard by the audience. Some drummers find a ringy head objectionable, not realizing that the ring is absorbed by the volume of other instruments and room acoustics, leaving only the fundamental pitch by the time it reaches the audience. In studio or live performance situations where volume is low or the drums are amplified, too much ring from the heads makes them too loud and difficult to record or amplify. Choosing a head for its thickness and tonal characteristics to suit the application gives the best results.

When choosing the combination of batter and resonator head for a specific drum, remember that the tonal characteristics of the resonator head can enhance or modify those of the batter head. A rule of thumb is to choose a resonator head of the same or lesser thickness than the batter head if you want to maintain or brighten the sound of the drum. If you prefer to dampen its sound, use a resonator head of greater thickness than the batter head. This applies to single-ply heads. Two-ply heads produce a much more pronounced deadening effect when used as resonator heads. Except in situations where extreme deadening of sound is desired, single-ply heads are the best choice for resonator side use. You can experiment by applying one or two pieces of duct tape to the surface of your resonator heads to hear the approximate effect of fitting a thicker head.

The variety of heads available gives you more than enough combinations of batter and resonator heads to try. Different types of drums may require different head choices. Most drummers prefer to have the same tonal characteristics (at different pitches) from each of their toms. Unless one tom needs its sound modified to match the others, the easiest way to achieve this is to use the same heads on all of them. This means using the same combination of batter and resonator heads on each drum, not necessarily the same type of head on batter and resonator side. Snare drums and bass drums are each designed to produce distinct tonal characteristics. They may also be subject to more consistent, heavy use than toms, as previously mentioned. To produce the sound you want, your choice of heads for snare or bass drums may be quite different from those best suited for use on toms.

If the heads you are using are giving you the sound you want, you can replace them with identical heads when they wear out. If you are unhappy with their sound and you have tried various ways of tuning and muffling without success, it is time to experiment with different heads. Experimentation with the preceding information in mind is the best way to learn. Let your ears and your personal preferences be the judge.

Modifying Drumheads

To obtain the sound of a single headed bass drum or tom without removing the resonator head and tuning hardware, cut a circular hole in the resonator head a few inches smaller than the shell diameter. The remaining perimeter portion of the head stays in place, protecting the bearing edge of the shell from damage. The drum will have the characteristic shorter sustain and increased projection of attack common to single headed drums.

Single headed drum sounds are not currently in fashion but it is common practice to modify the sound of a bass drum by cutting a somewhat smaller hole in the resonator head. Some drum manufacturers supply these vented or ported heads as standard equipment and you can also buy bass drum heads with vent holes from some drumhead manufacturers.

If you wish to experiment with this sound, use a compass or dividers to draw or scribe a circle in the head. The hole can be in the center of the head or offset from the center. Cut out the circle with a knife or scissors. The edge of the hole will be quite sharp. The larger the hole, the less resonant and more like a single headed bass drum the sound will be. The smaller the hole, the less effect it has on the sound. By starting with a 4″ or 5″ hole and listening to the difference it makes, you can increase the size of the hole by one or two inch increments until you find the tonal quality you want.

Even if you prefer the sound of a full resonator head on your bass drum, you may have to cut a hole in the head to permit the insertion of a microphone. If so, locate the hole away from the center of the head and restrict its size to 4″ or 5″. This will result in a very minor modification of the sound, still giving the drum the resonance of a full resonator head.

There are a couple of solutions to the problem of sharp or ragged looking edges in drumhead vent holes. To prevent cutting yourself when handling the drum and to prevent the edge of the vent hole from tearing, it can be reinforced and or covered. Some drumhead manufacturers, such as Aquarian, sell vented heads with a layer of reinforcing material surrounding the vent hole. If you cut your own hole, you can cover and reinforce the edge with an accessory product such as the Head Saver made by the Drum Guys. This self-adhesive, plastic trim can be cut to fit holes from 4" to 14" diameter. Its chrome-like finish dresses up the edge of the hole as well as protecting it from tearing.

It is also common practice for drummers to use their bass drum resonator heads as advertising billboards by painting their name or initials or the name of their band on them. If you watch old films that feature some of the early jazz bands, you will see landscapes or other scenes painted on bass drumheads. Covering the entire surface of the head with paint increases its thickness and slightly decreases its resonance. Sometimes that has a beneficial effect on the sound, but if this concerns you, you can compensate by using less muffling or no muffling at all on the resonator head or by starting with a thinner, more resonant head than you would normally use in this application.

Cleaning Drumheads

Drumheads get dusty and dirty and require occasional cleaning. Always remove a head from the drum to clean it and dry a plastic head thoroughly before re-fitting it. Calfskin heads can be washed with warm water and saddle soap, blotted dry with a towel and installed on the drum with light tension while still damp. Do not play a calfskin head until it has dried thoroughly. To prevent calfskin from drying out and cracking, an occasional, light application of leather preservative or silicone protectant such as Armor All might prove beneficial.

Plastic heads can be washed with a soft sponge, warm water and liquid dishwashing detergent. Rinse them thoroughly with water before drying. Remo Fiberskyn 2 heads can be wiped with a damp sponge, but soaking them in water or scrubbing them may destroy their coating. Rough textured heads pick up black marks from sticks and brushes that are particularly hard to remove. Powdered, abrasive household cleansers will scrub off all but the most stubborn marks. This also wears away some of the rough coating, however, making the head less effective for brush work.

Drum Tuning and Muffling

There is probably no other subject that causes so much confusion and disagreement among drummers as the tuning of drums. While most other competent musicians know how to tune their instruments, it is quite common to find experienced drummers who do not understand drum tuning.

There are a few reasons for this. First, there is no single, standardized, accepted sound for the drums in a drumset. Drums are tuned according to the taste of the drummer and the requirements of the music being performed. Second, drums are not considered definite-pitch instruments. They produce a fundamental pitch and a range of overtones. This allows their sound to blend with any note or chord being played by other instruments, but it also makes them difficult to tune by ear with clarity. Third, many drummers receive little or no instruction in tuning technique.

Poor quality drum sound and the lack of knowledge to correct it perpetuates the myth that drummers are second class musicians. Careful attention to tuning and muffling makes even the least expensive drumset sound better. Your drums are the backbone of the rhythm section. When they sound good, they inspire the other musicians and make the whole band sound better.

Tuning

There are as many possible variations of drum sounds as there are drummers. Properly tuned drums sound musical and complementary to the other instruments in the intended musical application. You will develop your own preferences in sound by experimenting.

In order to get the best results from tuning, a drum must be in good condition with all parts of its tuning hardware clean and lubricated, as explained in the section of this book on drum maintenance. The drumheads must not be worn out. Over-stretched head collars and dents in the playing surface make it very difficult to tune a head precisely.

Tuning a drum consists of tensioning the heads and muffling them if necessary to achieve the fundamental pitch, tonal quality and stick response you want. Because a drumset consists of several drums, tuning also involves harmonious pitch separation between drums and consistent tonal quality among toms. The most basic concept of tuning is that the greater the tension applied to the head, the higher the fundamental pitch it produces. The lower the tension, the lower the fundamental pitch. In addition to this, higher tension produces faster stick response (more bounce), while lower tension produces slower stick response.

Remember that every drumshell is capable of being tuned to a certain range of pitch, dependent on its dimensions. A large drum can only be tuned so high and a small drum only so low before the sound quality will suffer. Choose your drum sizes to suit the pitch range you have in mind.

The following list of drumshell diameters shows the approximate number of square inches of playing surface on a head fitted to that size of shell:

Diameter shell		Square inches
6"	=	28
8"	=	50
10"	=	79
12"	=	113
13"	=	133
14"	=	154
15"	=	177
16"	=	201
18"	=	254
20"	=	314
22"	=	380
24"	=	452
26"	=	531

This list should make it obvious why heads of only a few inches difference in diameter can have very different tonal properties. A few inches more or less in diameter can mean a substantial difference in surface area.

Another basic concept that is at the root of many tuning problems is the need for even head tension. Regardless of the amount of tension applied, if it is not applied evenly over the entire surface of the head, the head will not be in tune with itself. This makes the fundamental pitch unclear and creates discordant overtones.

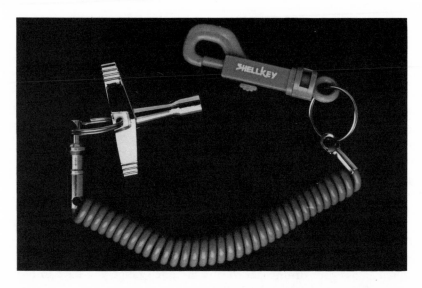

Shellkey is a drum tuning key that clips to a tension rod or other hardware. This prevents loss of the key and keeps it handy. *(Courtesy of Shellkey/Michael Richards.)*

Therefore, the primary goal in tuning a drum is to get the head in tune with itself by setting tension evenly at each tension point. Then you can raise or lower the pitch according to your preference and use muffling where necessary to modify the tonal quality. The procedure for setting even tension is identical for bass drums, snare drums and toms.

Drums are tuned with tuning keys, which are really small, chrome plated sockets with t-handles at the top for turning by hand. The socket fits the square-headed (or occasionally slot-headed) tension rods. The tension rods on bass drums may have t-handles instead of square heads, allowing you to turn them by hand instead of using a key. Keys are small, but important items that are easily lost. They are available at most music stores and it is wise to keep a few spares on hand.

A useful device for preventing loss and keeping a tuning key handy while performing is the Shellkey, a tuning key attached to a curly extension cord with a clip at the end. The cord can be clipped onto a tension rod or other part of the set, allowing you to use the key on any drum while the cord is still attached. This is a simple idea that can save you from hunting for a key when you have some fine tuning to do during a performance. When removing or installing drumheads, you can save time by using a rachet-action key instead of a regular tuning key. An example of this type of device is the Pro-Mark Ratch-It. The rachet device is reversible for clockwise or counter-clockwise use and has a locked position for fine tuning.

It also has a slot head/ Phillips screwdriver bit for loosening or tightening snare cord attachment points or other fasteners. Unlike some rachet or "speed" keys, its handle is not offset from the socket, making it quite smooth and stable to use.

Start the tuning procedure by placing the drum on a padded surface (a pillow or blanket is good) with the head you are going to tune facing up. The padded surface muffles the opposite head, allowing you to hear clearly the sound of the head on which you are working. You will need a drum tuning key to tune and a drumstick to tap the head.

The drum should be fully assembled as explained in the drum maintenance

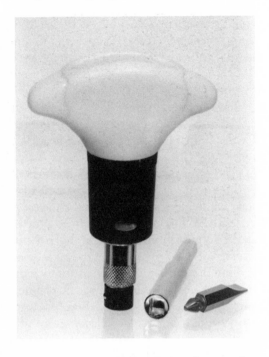

Pro-Mark Ratch-It is a ratcheting drum tuning key that speeds up head installation or removal. The extra slot head/Phillips bit is useful for jobs requiring a screwdriver. *(Courtesy of Pro-Mark Corp.)*

section of this book. The head and counterhoop are in position with the tension rods only finger tight. When fitting a new head, remember to align the trademark on the head with the trademark on the shell. That makes it easy to replace the head in the same position if it is removed. This is important because heads conform to the contour of the drumshell when tensioned and are easier to re-tune when fitted in the same position.

The head must be seated on the shell before it can be evenly tuned. Seating a head is a stretching procedure that makes the head conform to the exact contour of the bearing edge. Place your tuning key on each tension rod and turn them one-half turn clockwise. Use a crisscross pattern, moving from one tension rod to the rod diametrically opposite. Using two tuning keys to turn opposite rods at the same time is an excellent idea. You may have to repeat this until any slack or ripples are removed from the head. Place the palm of your hand in the center of the head and press down firmly. Be gentle with snare heads, as they are more delicate than other types of heads. You may hear cracking sounds if you are using heads with glued construction. As long as the head material does not pull out of the hoop, there is no cause for concern. When you release the pressure of your hand, the head may have slack in it again. Repeat the tensioning procedure until there is no slack in the head. It is now seated on the shell and ready to tune.

With your drumstick, tap the head near each tension rod about one or two inches from the edge. Try to ignore any high pitched ring and listen for the fundamental pitch of the head. Use your key to raise the pitch by tightening (turn clockwise) or lower the pitch by loosening (turn counter-clockwise) so that the head produces the same fundamental pitch at each tension point. If you eventually want to tune the drum to a lower pitch, start at the tension point with the lowest pitch and adjust all the others to match it. If you eventually want to tune the drum to a higher pitch, start at the tension point with the highest pitch and adjust all the others to match it. Use a crisscross method from one tension rod to the opposite one, turning the key in one-quarter turn increments. If you were to work around the drum from one tension rod to the next in the early stages, you could end up with the head pulled down unevenly at one side. Adjusting tension at each point affects the tension at all other points. Working on tension points diametrically opposite each other keeps the head more evenly seated. Turning the key in small increments also prevents the head from being pulled to one side.

It may take several times through the crisscross pattern before you are satisfied that all tension points are producing the same fundamental pitch. This is the most confusing part of tuning and takes a little practice. You must train your ear to hear slight variances in pitch.

A useful trick when you have trouble hearing pitch differences is tapping the head as you loosen and then tighten the tension rod by one-half turn. Hearing the pitch change as you tap the head makes it more audible for comparison with the other tension points.

Now you can adjust the pitch of the head higher or lower by turning each tension rod an equal amount clockwise or counter-clockwise. Use the crisscross pattern and do not turn any tension rod more than one-quarter turn at a time. Check each tension point for even pitch when you have reached the tension you want and fine tune any that are slightly high or low.

The next step is to turn the drum over and repeat the whole procedure on the opposite head. Because of the nature of head material, a new head often requires re-tuning after a short break-in period. After that, it should require only periodic checks to see that it is staying in tune. When it begins to require frequent re-tuning that still does not restore its sound quality and stick response, it is time to replace the head.

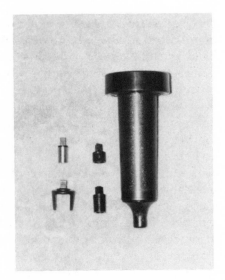

Left: The Neary Drum-Torque, a tool for measuring drumhead tension, tunes drums to precise, even tension and pitch scientifically. *Right:* Side view of the Neary Drum-Torque, showing interchangeable bits for different tension rods or bass drum t-handles. *(Courtesy of Neary Industries, Ltd.)*

The only difficulty with this tuning method is that it relies on your ears to sense pitch differences. After many years of practice, some drummers can tune by the feel of the key on the rod, without striking the head until they reach the fine tuning stage. The resistance they feel at each rod guides them. Other drummers never develop confidence in their ability to hear subtle pitch differences. For them, tuning is a frustrating process of tapping, listening and adjusting that often ends in ear fatigue, confusion and poor results.

If tuning is difficult for you or if you would like a quicker, simpler way of doing it, there is a solution to the problem. Drummers can use a simple tool that measures head tension without listening to the drum. An example of this type of tool is the Neary Drum-Torque.

When you tune a drum with a key, you are applying torque to the tension rods. This pulls the head tighter across the shell, raising the pitch. The Neary Drum-Torque is a torque measuring tool. Instead of listening to the pitch of the drum, it measures the amount of torque applied at each tension point. Even tension around the head creates even pitch. Setting each tension rod at the same torque measurement puts the head precisely in tune.

The Drum-Torque is capable of tuning faster and with greater precision than most drummers' ears. It requires clean, well lubricated, undamaged tension rods and threaded inserts in order to work properly. Any mechanical friction between the moving parts of the drum's tuning hardware will create a false, high torque reading. After you complete the procedures outlined in this book in the section on drum maintenance, a Drum-Torque should work perfectly on your drums.

Once each head is in tune with itself, you must consider the relative tension between the batter head and the resonator head of each drum. In the larger context of the whole drumset, you must consider the pitch relationship between drums. Although bass drums and snare drums are tuned to produce separate tonal characteristics, the toms should be similar in tone with harmonious pitch intervals between them.

This is a part of tuning that is often neglected or done poorly. Setting pitch intervals by ear is as difficult for some drummers as setting even tension on a head. The result is a drumset with no clear difference in pitch between the toms or a jarring, discordant interval from one tom to another. It is not always understood that striking one drum creates sympathetic vibrations in all the others. If there is no pleasing harmonic pitch relationship between them, striking any drum will create discordant overtones that detract from the sound quality of the whole drumset.

This is another application where a tuning tool such as the Neary Drum-Torque can save you time and effort. Its instruction book provides examples of various combinations of toms with recommended torque readings for each drum. Following the instructions results in equal, harmonious pitch intervals between toms. Unfortunately, not all possible drumset configurations can be covered in the instruction book.

The relative tension between the batter and resonator heads of a drum may also be set by ear or by Drum-Torque. There are three options. Both heads may be tuned to the same pitch, the batter head may be tuned to a higher pitch or the resonator head may be tuned to a higher pitch. Any of these methods is acceptable. Be aware of the fact that equal tension between heads will produce equal pitch only if the heads are of the same type and thickness. Heads of different type or thickness may produce unequal pitch at the same level of tension.

When setting relative head tension, remember that it is just as important to maintain a pleasing harmonic relationship between the batter head and resonator head as it is to maintain a similar relationship between the pitches of different drums. That is not a problem if both heads are tuned to the same pitch. If one head is tuned to a higher pitch than the other, be sure that the interval between them is not discordant.

One factor that influences the relative tension you use is your requirement for bounce or stick response from the batter heads of snare drums and toms. If you prefer a simple playing style, you do not need the fast stick response provided by high batter head tension. The fewer notes you play, the more the drum can sustain for a legato effect. This is best achieved by low to medium batter head tension. If you prefer a busier, more technical playing style, you require faster stick response. The more notes you play, the shorter the sound should sustain for a staccato effect. A shorter sustain gives better definition to each stroke so your fast rhythmic patterns are not lost in a rumble of sound. This is best achieved by medium to high batter head tension. Bass drum batter head tension has less effect on your technique. The foot pedal return spring can provide some of the response regardless of head tension.

Following from this, you may wish to set the batter heads of your toms at a level of tension that gives you the desired stick response and tonal quality. Their pitch can then be modified somewhat by raising or lowering the tension of the resonator heads (remembering to maintain a pleasing pitch interval). This effect is limited because the resonator head influences the tonal characteristics of a drum more than its pitch.

The difference in feel between the hard surface of a cymbal and a loosely tuned drumhead may require a variance in grip or technique when moving from one to the other. If you like the pitch of your drums low, try selecting a head that produces relatively low pitch at reasonably firm tension. As an alternative, use larger diameter or deeper drums that can produce low pitch when firmly tensioned. Either solution can improve your speed and reduce effort and fatigue.

A drum with batter and resonator heads tuned to the same pitch produces a more consistent fundamental pitch. In addition, the dimensions and other construction factors of a drum tend to make it most resonant at a particular pitch. Experimenting with head tension can lead to the discovery of this optimal pitch for each drum.

If you wish to test the idea of shell resonance to its extreme, you can disassemble a drum and tap the bare shell to hear the pitch it produces. Make note of this pitch, reassemble the drum and tune both heads to that pitch. Theoretically, with all components vibrating at the same frequency, this should be the most resonant pitch with the smallest amount of discordant overtones. Unfortunately, creating a very strong fundamental pitch from a drum and minimizing its overtones makes it possible for the drum to sound out of tune with the rest of the band if they are playing a note or chord that conflicts with the fundamental pitch of the drum. Some overtones are desirable to allow the drum to blend harmoniously with other instruments.

The snare drum is traditionally the high pitched voice of the drumset. Regardless of its nominal pitch, the snares give it a sharper, crisper tonal quality than a tom or bass drum. You may use your snare drum at times with the snares disengaged from the head, especially if you play any Latin dance music. In this case, the pitch interval between your snare drum and toms should be set carefully to avoid a discordant effect. Tuning a snare drum to achieve good snare response is slightly more complex than tuning a bass drum or tom.

Because of the significant difference in thickness between batter and snare heads, there is confusion about which head should be tighter or higher pitched. A snare head may produce a different pitch than the batter head even though it has the same tension applied to it, because it is so thin.

Snare drum batter heads may be tensioned high for brighter, crisper sound or low for deeper, warmer sound. Within limits, the same can be said for snare heads, but outside a fairly narrow range of adjustment, the snare response will suffer. Snare heads tensioned too tightly are unable to vibrate freely, producing a choked sound. Snare heads that are too loose produce a tubby, flabby sound. Poor snare drum sound is often caused by one of these two extremes. In my experience, the problem is usually not enough tension. Careful experimentation will determine the correct range of snare head tension on your snare drum.

Adjustment of snare tension and snare contact with the head has a significant effect on the sound of a snare drum. On most drums, both of these adjustments are actuated in unison by the snare tension adjustment control. On more sophisticated snare mechanisms, snare tension and snare contact with the head can be adjusted independently.

To test your snare head for proper response, tap around the edge of the batter head. The snares should respond clearly right to the edge of the head. Strike the batter head in the center and half way between the center and the edge. Listen for excessive rattle or a tight, choked sound. The snares should respond freely at all volume levels. Try a buzz roll (press roll, multiple bounce roll) to see if you get the response you need.

Too much tension on the snares or too tight contact between the snares and the snare head will choke the drum. Although the snare head may be tensioned properly, the snares may be too tight to respond to vibrations or they may be pressing too much on the head, muffling the vibration. The opposite extreme is a rattly, loose sound that obscures the definition of each stroke during fast rhythmic patterns. This is caused by insufficient snare tension and or incomplete contact between the snares and snare head.

The difference between a great sounding snare drum and one that is choked or rattly can be as little as a quarter turn of the snare tension adjustment control. To adjust the snares correctly if you have a sophisticated snare mechanism, you first adjust snare tension to a moderate setting so you can adjust the contact of the snares with the head. Contact must be level all across the head without exerting excessive pressure on the head at either end. Then continue with the following instructions for adjusting snare tension.

If you have a standard snare mechanism, start with the snare throw-off control in the "on" position and the snares loose. Strike the drum repeatedly mid-way between edge and center, tightening the snare tension by one-quarter turn increments every few strokes. As the snares tighten, the drum

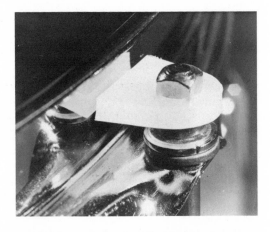

Lug Locks are nylon locking devices that press onto tension rods to prevent de-tuning. *(Courtesy of L.T. Lug Lock, Inc.)*

reaches a point where it sounds particularly alive and sensitive. Continue past this point until the snares begin to choke, then reverse the adjustment gradually until you reach the "live" adjustment range again. Finish by testing snare response at different volume levels all over the batter head, as previously described.

Drums have a tendency to go out of tune due to vibration as you play them. This is a constant problem for heavy players, especially on snare drums when you play a heavy back-beat or frequent rim shots.

Tension rods can actually vibrate loose during heavy playing. Loud rim shots depress the batter side counterhoop, allowing the tension rods to rotate. Vibration even loosens the tension rods on the resonator head. The less tension you use to begin with, the more frequently you will have to re-tune. Higher tension puts more stress and friction on the tuning hardware, which allows it to resist the loosening effects of vibration longer.

Some manufacturers offer lock nuts for their snare drum tension rods to correct this problem. Another alternative is to use Lug Locks, made by L.T. Lug Lock. Lug Locks are small pieces of plastic with a rounded edge, a flat edge and a hole in the middle. After you have tuned a drum, position a Lug Lock so that its flat edge faces the upright portion of the counterhoop, with the round hole of the Lug Lock over the square head of the tension rod. Press the Lug Lock onto the head of the tension rod. Friction holds it in place on the tension rod and its flat edge against the counterhoop keeps the tension rod from rotating. When you need to adjust tuning or replace a drumhead, pop the Lug Lock off the tension rod with your fingers or the end of a drumstick.

Lug Locks can be re-used many times and are inexpensive. The plastic can be trimmed to fit against thicker die cast counterhoops if necessary. You may want to use them on every tension rod or only on the batter and snare side of your snare drum, close to where you strike the counterhoop for rim shots. Lug Locks will not work on round-headed tension rods such as the ones found on Sonor drums or older Premier drums. Sonor uses a patented "Snap Lock" anti-rotation device that is built into the tuning hardware of their drums to prevent them from going out of tune due to vibration. Premier drums have been equipped with standard, square-headed tension rods for many years.

Muffling

Muffling the sound of a drum may be necessary in some situations to modify its tonal quality or reduce its volume. Muffling reduces the amount of high pitched overtones that the drum produces, putting more emphasis on the fundamental pitch.

Ideally, in situations where there is no amplification or recording involved, drums should be played with little or no muffling. This creates a full, resonant sound that can cut through the volume of other instruments and be heard clearly at a distance. A common fault among inexperienced drummers is the use of excessive muffling.

To the drummer sitting at the drumset, an unmuffled drum may sound harsh and ringy. The assumption is that it sounds the same way to the audience, so muffling is applied until the drum sounds warm and mellow at a distance of two feet. Now the drum sounds good to the drummer but unless amplification is used, it probably will not be heard at all in the audience. By damping all of the high pitched ring from the drum, you drastically reduce its volume and projection.

The point is, a ringy drum does not sound ringy to the audience. Much of the ring is absorbed by the sound of other instruments, audience noise and room acoustics. What reaches the ears of the audience is the warm, mellow sound you want them to hear. When tuning and muffling, it is important to keep in mind this difference in perception of sound from stage and audience perspectives. It will help you to judge just how much muffling is necessary in a given acoustic situation.

A completely open, unmuffled sound is not always desirable or even appropriate for certain musical styles or acoustic situations. For example, in recording studios or during live performances when the drums are amplified, too much ring creates problems for the recording engineer or sound technician. Acoustic drums are difficult instruments to record or

amplify because of the high volume of their attack sound and the wide range of overtones they produce. A microphone over or inside each drum makes acoustic volume and projection unnecessary, so the overtones can be muffled without reducing the sound heard by the audience or recorded on the tape.

Before the 1970s, resonant-sounding drums were fashionable. Then the tendency to muffle drums heavily in recording studios began to

Shure microphone used on snare drum. Close miking often requires some muffling to produce good results. *(Courtesy of Shure Brothers.)*

influence the sound that drummers wanted in live situations. Advances in recording technology and the inevitable changes in "fashionable" drum sound have made resonant-sounding drums popular again.

In live performance where no amplification is used, muffling is helpful to compensate for a room with poor acoustics or to reduce volume for very quiet performances. It is easier to muffle the sound of your drums than to hold back and radically alter your playing technique when too much volume is a concern.

Selecting the appropriate type of heads and tuning for the tonal quality you want will reduce the amount of muffling you require. In the days of calfskin heads, many drums were supplied without muffling devices. Early plastic heads produced more ring than calfskin, so internal mufflers or "tone controls" quickly became standard equipment. They consist of felt pads attached to metal arms. An external knob or lever on the drumshell moves the felt pad into contact with the underside of the batter head. You may also find drums with internal tone controls fitted for the resonator heads.

Internal tone controls are still standard equipment on some snare drums, although they have fallen out of fashion entirely for toms. Their main drawback is a tendency to rattle when you strike the drum, especially when the felt pad is not in contact with the head. Some designs are worse than others in this respect. It is quite common to find older drums with the internal tone controls removed.

The proper way to use an internal tone control is to adjust the position of the felt pad so that its entire surface contacts the underside of the head without pressing against it. This gives the maximum reduction of overtones. Less contact provides less muffling but tighter contact against the head actually reduces its effectiveness and creates discordant overtones by distorting the head. Experiment by tapping the head as you adjust the tone control. You will hear when you reach the point of diminishing returns.

The main reason cited for the elimination of most internal tone controls is their restriction of batter head movement. Because they are under the head, they get in the way of the downward movement of the head when it is struck. In extreme cases, this can choke the sound of the head. Using internal tone controls properly, as described, minimizes this problem.

An alternative muffling idea that avoids these problems is the external tone control. This device clips onto the drum's counterhoop, positioning an adjustable felt pad on top of the head. When the head is struck, it depresses and returns to position without interference from the external muffler. The only disadvantage to this device is that it takes up space on the head and can get in the way, particularly for a drummer who uses brushes.

External mufflers were hailed as a new idea in the mid–1970s, but they were really a recycling of an old idea. Large ones were widely used as bass drum mufflers in the first decades of the twentieth century. They can be seen in many photographs of old drumsets.

The old, temporary method of muffling a snare drum or tom is to place your wallet, cigarette package or similar object at the edge of the batter head.

There are several other expedient methods of muffling toms and snare drums. Duct tape is often applied to heads to reduce ring but it is more effective if it is used to tape a small, folded piece of soft material (such as cloth, paper toweling or felt) to the edge of the head. This is usually taped on top of the head, making it easy to remove or modify. If you tape anything to the underside of the head, you will have to cope with the nuisance of removing the head each time you want to alter the muffling to suit different room acoustics. Occasionally, felt strips are placed under the head, but these are inconvenient for the same reason. Generally, felt

Remo Muff'ls use a plastic tray and foam donut or disk under the head to muffle head ring. *(Courtesy of Remo, Inc.)*

strips under the heads of toms and snare drums muffle too much and can cause buzzing sounds if they pass under the middle of the head.

Because most high pitched overtones are generated near the edge of the drumhead, most muffling devices are applied to this area. Self-adhesive foam weatherstripping is sometimes stuck to the perimeter of the head. Varying the amount of perimeter area covered this way regulates the desired amount of resonance. Removal and re-application of this material is not usually an easy process. Deadringer is the name of a commercially available version of this muffling method.

Some drummers construct a device similar to a timpani mute. A piece of felt, suede leather or folded paper towel is taped to the counterhoop and rests on the batter head. It can be flipped on or off the head as needed. Because it is not attached to the head, it bounces when the head is struck, immediately muffling the after-ring.

Remo manufactures a product called Muff'ls in sizes for snare drums, toms or bass drums. It comes in two variations, Ring Control or Sound Control and requires head removal to install or remove. It consists of a plastic ring that fits over the bearing edge of the shell under the head. The ring has a channel in it around the edge of the head. By using the plastic ring alone, some degree of muffling is achieved. The Ring Control kit contains a piece of foam rubber that fits into the plastic ring under the head, producing a more muffled effect. The Sound Control kit contains a disc-shaped piece of foam rubber that covers the underside of the head, held in place by the plastic ring. This has a serious deadening effect on the drum. Another disc of foam rubber may be placed inside the drum resting

Noble & Cooley Zero Rings are flat Mylar plastic "donuts" used for muffling drumhead ring. *(Courtesy of Noble & Cooley Drum Company.)*

on the underside of the resonator head. Using both discs not only dampens the resonance of the drum, it drastically reduces its volume.

Sound Control Muff'ls are useful for quiet practice on your drumset. The Ring Control version can be used for live performance or studio recording, remembering that any alteration of the degree of muffling will require the removal of the drumhead. One disadvantage of this device is that the plastic ring covers the bearing edge of the shell and in effect replaces the bearing edge. Another problem is the tendency of the plastic ring to crack at the point where it touches the bearing edge of the shell. This necessitates rather frequent replacement of the Muff'ls, an unnecessary expense.

Perhaps the most versatile method of muffling snare drums and toms is to cut a ring of plastic from an old drumhead. It should fit the perimeter of the head you wish to muffle and be as wide as needed. The more of the head that is covered from the edge toward the middle, the greater the muffling effect. Try a one inch width to start. If this muffles too much, you can cut the ring into two pieces and use only a semicircle. If you need more muffling, try wider rings in increments of one-half inch.

This type of muffling device is available commercially from several companies. One example is the Noble & Cooley Drum Company, who call their product Zero Rings. The advantage of the commercially-made rings is that they are completely flat, unlike a section cut from an old head that may not lie flat. They are available in several sizes. When even more muffling is required, they can be stacked on top of one another. One disadvantage is the tendency of drumsticks or (particularly) brushes to catch under a ring and lift it off the head during a performance. Although they function best when resting loosely

The Fattner is a Mylar plastic disk that muffles ring and deepens the tone of a snare drum when placed on the batter head. *(Courtesy of Timeline Products.)*

on the head, taping them to the head at two or three spots can minimize this problem. The Evans drumhead company manufactures a line of heads with integral muffling rings under the playing surface. This has the advantage of keeping them out of the way, but renders them nonadjustable.

To muffle and significantly deepen the sound of a snare drum or tom, you can cut out a plastic disc (from an old drumhead) that covers the whole head you are trying to muffle. Playing on this surface is more difficult, as stick response is noticeably decreased and brush work will not be heard clearly. However, placing a disc of this type on top of a drum can give you a quick change of tonal quality when you want to produce the deep, heavily processed sound heard on many records. A commercial example of this idea is the Fattner, from Timeline Products. It is a set of two identical discs designed for use on the snare drum. Made from a thicker plastic than you would usually get by cutting up an old drumhead, it lies flat on the batter head to make it easier to play on. The use of two discs, one on top of the other can make a 5″ deep snare drum sound like a 10″ deep drum, but also reduces volume too much for some circumstances.

Completely unmuffled bass drums are too boomy for many drummers' tastes. Minimal damping of the ringy sound can be achieved with some form of impact pad attached to the striking area of the batter head. It has the added benefit of absorbing some of the wear in this heavily stressed area. A layer of drumhead material can be taped to the head to slightly dampen overtones while emphasizing the attack click of the stroke. Self-adhesive fabric impact pads with a hard disc in the center, such as the Super Rock pad from Danmar, do the same thing. Impact pads that emphasize the attack click are particularly useful for recording or for live performances using microphones for amplification.

For a softer attack sound and for lighter players, an impact pad made from material similar in texture to wool felt is good. Self-adhesive "moleskin" can be purchased in the foot care section of most pharmacies and cut to the size you need. I normally use a patch approximately 3″ or 4″ square. When it wears smooth, I remove it and stick on a new piece.

Somewhat more muffling can be achieved without completely deadening the bass drum. The old standby of a felt strip under the batter (and sometimes the resonator) head will cut much of the ring and objectionable boominess. Felt strips can be purchased at most music store drum departments. Place them horizontally or vertically across the end of the shell, staying several inches away from the center to avoid buzzing noises. One strip under each head is usually sufficient and some drummers are satisfied with a felt strip under the batter head only.

The previously mentioned Remo Ring Control Muff'l kit is more practical for bass drums than snares or toms. Using a Ring Control Muff'l on the batter head (with or without a felt strip on the resonator head) is a simple way to produce a powerful sound with very little ring. Depending on the degree of muffling desired, you can try using only the plastic ring of the Muff'l kit without the foam ring. A friend of mine found that he got the best results for his circumstances by cutting the foam ring into two semi-circles and using only half of it in the plastic ring. There is plenty of room for experimentation here to achieve the effect you want.

The traditional, counterhoop-mounted, external bass drum tone control is still available from companies such as Danmar Percussion Products and has the advantage of being instantly adjustable without removing the head. Some drum companies offer internal tone controls for bass drums that are externally adjustable. Two examples are Sonor and Gretsch. Installation of either of these internal tone controls should be considered permanent, as it involves drilling holes in the bass drumshell.

Most drummers are familiar with the use of pillows, blankets, slabs of foam rubber and other sound-absorbing materials stuffed inside the shell to deaden the sound of a bass drum. They are placed in contact with both the batter head and the resonator head and have a severe muffling effect. Even in recording studios, this much muffling is not really necessary if the engineer is knowledgeable and takes the time to do things properly. Unfortunately, in imitation of the dead "thump" sound of bass drums on many recordings, it has become standard procedure for many drummers doing live performances as well. This stuffing of the bass drum is often combined with the full or partial removal of the bass drum resonator head for an even deader sound.

When the use of a microphone is not a concern, use only as much bass drum muffling as you really need. Keep in mind that sound with no resonance will not carry clearly into the audience. More careful head selection and tuning, combined with some of the other muffling techniques could result in clear, pleasant bass drum sounds.

The same advice applies to your snare drum and toms. Use discretion when muffling any drum and experiment with different methods to find the one that best suits your circumstances.

Drumsticks, Brushes, Mallets and Beaters

The striking implements commonly used to play the drumset are drumsticks, brushes and mallets. The beaters of bass drum foot pedals are also mallets designed for their special application.

The particular stick, brush, mallet or beater you choose affects the volume level and tonal quality produced by the drum or cymbal it strikes. It also affects your playing technique by the way it reacts against a drumhead or cymbal. Any well stocked music store has a wide variety of these products. Selecting the appropriate size and type of stick, brush or mallet for your application will make them last longer and help you get the volume and tone you want while improving your playing technique. Random selection without considering the following information often results in unnecessary playing difficulties, inappropriate sound and frequent breakage.

Drumsticks

In order to choose the appropriate model of drumstick for the application, you must first be familiar with the variables in drumstick design. Each part of a drumstick is subject to variations in size and shape. The following terms are used for the parts of a drumstick: tip or bead, neck, shoulder or taper, shank or shaft, butt.

The tip or bead is at the forward end of the stick. This is the part of the stick designed to strike the drum or cymbal in most circumstances. Immediately behind it is the neck, which is usually the thinnest part of the stick. One reason for the neck being thin is to allow the tip to strike almost parallel to the surface of a cymbal or drumhead without the rest of the stick

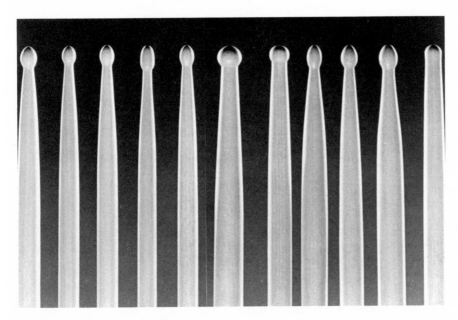

Regal wood tip drumsticks, showing variations of dimension in tips, necks, tapers, and shank thickness. *(Courtesy of Calato Manufacturing.)*

interfering (physically or acoustically). Behind the neck is the shoulder or taper, where the stick increases in size to its full diameter. Behind this is the shank or shaft of the stick, which gives it the desired length. The back end of the stick is the butt, which is occasionally used for striking.

Most drumsticks are made of wood. Metal and synthetic material drumsticks are also available. Although wood tends to break or wear out faster than the synthetic materials currently in use, it has characteristics of sound, feel and response that have not yet been precisely imitated. Instead of judging modern synthetic sticks by their ability to imitate the characteristics of wood, they should be regarded as an alternate choice of material that may be more suitable in certain circumstances.

The most commonly used types of wood for drumsticks sold in North America are hickory, maple and oak. Different grades and sub-species of these woods are used by different manufacturers, but a general comparison can be made. The density of maple is lower than that of hickory. Hickory has a lower density than oak. Therefore, if you pick up identically sized drumsticks made from each of these woods, the maple stick will be the lightest, the hickory stick will be heavier and the oak stick will be the heaviest. Disregarding other considerations for the moment, this allows you to choose the physical size of stick you like and vary the weight by using different materials. Alternately, you can use sticks of

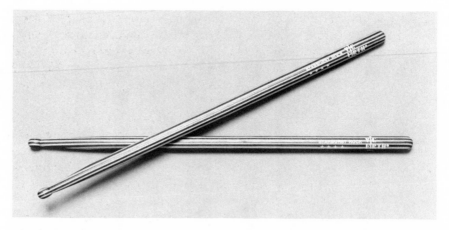

**Vic Firth Starburst series sticks, made from different colored laminations of maple.
This cosmetic striped effect doesn't wear off because it is part of the wood.
*(Courtesy of Vic Firth, Inc.)***

different sizes and stay within the weight range you prefer by varying the
type of wood.

Different wood density and weight create additional characteristics.
All wooden sticks gradually dent, chip and wear away with use. Other factors being equal, a maple stick will have a faster wear rate than a hickory
or oak stick. Maple feels slightly softer and more flexible against a cymbal
or drumhead. Being softer, it soaks up more of the perceived shock of striking a hard surface. Being lighter, a maple stick produces a slightly thinner
tonal quality from a drum or cymbal than hickory or oak. Lighter sticks require less effort to use, but may require more forceful playing to produce
high volume.

Some maple sticks are not made from a solid piece of maple but from
several laminations, giving them longitudinal stripes. Ludwig claims that
their Powerline laminated maple sticks are stronger than a regular maple
stick while remaining relatively light in weight. Starburst series laminated
maple sticks from Vic Firth are made with alternating colored laminations for cosmetic purposes only. They claim no extra strength from this
process.

Hickory, being harder than maple, has more resistance to wear. It is
still soft enough to feel resilient, but transmits slightly more shock to the
drummer's hands. Hickory produces a somewhat fuller, more solid tonal
quality from drums and cymbals than maple, due to its increased density
and weight. For heavier players, this, plus its durability advantage, offsets
the extra effort required to manipulate a heavier stick.

Oak, being the hardest of these three woods, has the greatest resistance to wear. It also has the least resilience and transmits more of the shock of a stroke to the hand than either maple or hickory. Oak produces the most solid tonal quality and greatest volume of the three woods from drumheads and cymbals, which can be an advantage for the heavy player. However, its increased weight and lower resilience may require greater effort to use, depending on your playing technique.

The above-mentioned characteristics of different wood types affect the way they feel in your hand, the way they rebound from the surface of a drumhead or cymbal and consequently, the way you play. The differences are subtle and the way they are perceived is subjective. The best way to decide which type of wood is best for a given application is to try a pair of each type in identical sizes.

Synthetic drumsticks are usually molded from some form of plastic. The higher density of plastic (when compared to wood) makes some synthetic sticks feel exceptionally heavy for their size. Design innovations such as the hollow, tubular sticks from Aquarian Accessories overcome this problem to a great extent. Tubular construction has the added advantage of being stronger than solid material. Aquarian sticks also have a percentage of graphite in some of their models. Graphite reinforces the plastic, adding strength and resilience.

Aside from the greater strength and durability of some synthetic sticks, they have other advantages. Synthetic materials do not usually warp. Their method of construction allows precise uniformity of size, shape and weight. The greater density of the material creates a louder, more solid sound than the same size of wood stick, which can be useful for heavy players. Drummers who are accustomed to using wooden drumsticks may find that a period of adjustment is necessary before they feel comfortable with the slightly different response and rebound characteristics of synthetic sticks.

Before wooden sticks are made, the wood must be air and or kiln dried to a specific moisture content. Strong, straight sticks will result only if the moisture content is carefully monitored. Too little moisture makes the wood brittle, while too much results in warpage. Some companies keep their moisture content a trade secret, while others mention figures of 10 to 15 percent. Rimshot America advertises a moisture content of no more than 6 percent in their hickory drumsticks. Since every manufacturer seems to have their own idea of the ideal moisture content, experimentation and personal preference are your best guide when considering this feature.

The wood is shaped on a lathe, sanded and usually sealed against moisture with a clear lacquer or colored finish. You can buy wooden drumsticks with one of three levels of surface finish: bare, unsealed wood; satin finish (a thin sealant that feels similar to bare wood); and gloss finish (a thicker sealant with a shiny surface). Each manufacturer tends to choose one of these levels of finish for all of their sticks. An exception to this is Pro-Mark, who offer some of their drumstick models in both sealed and unsealed finish. Bare, unsealed wood is the finish most susceptible to moisture absorption and warpage. It may also wear away faster than sealed wood, especially at the tip. However, these are relatively minor problems. What works best for you and feels best in your hands is certainly a more significant consideration. Some drummers compromise by sanding off the lacquer sealant on the part of the stick that they grip. They feel that the slightly rougher texture of bare wood is less likely to slip out of their perspiring hands during a performance.

Colored finishes on drumsticks exist purely for cosmetic reasons. They have no functional benefits but they can add some visual flash to a performance. There are a couple of minor disadvantages to some colored sticks. The painted ones will eventually chip, making the sticks look more obviously worn than used sticks with a natural finish. The stained or dyed ones may leave colored marks on your cymbals and drumheads. The color of some synthetic drumsticks is part of the material, which avoids these problems. If you like the look of colored sticks, be sure to select the correct size and type for your application.

At each step of the manufacturing process, makers of better quality products inspect the sticks for defects and reject any with flaws that might affect their durability, appearance or proper function. High reject rates increase costs, which accounts for the high price of top quality drumsticks. Some manufacturers discard all sticks that do not meet their quality standards, while others offer a line of lower priced sticks that are not quite good enough to carry the first quality brand name. Some of these sticks have been rejected for reasons of appearance only and can be a good bargain. But make your selection very carefully to avoid any with serious flaws.

Before the sticks are packaged, quality manufacturers match each pair by weight. Wood is a natural material, so drumsticks of the same size and wood type may vary in density. Different density creates slightly different weight. When one drumstick in a pair is slightly heavier than the other, they feel unbalanced and produce different sounds on a drum or cymbal. Unfortunately, many music stores waste this matching procedure by removing the sticks from their plastic bags and placing several loose pairs together in a display bin. A minority of drummers actually prefer sticks of different weight in each hand. To allow mixing and matching of weight, most bags used for stick packaging are open-ended, allowing the customer to inspect the product before purchase.

Joe Calato invented the nylon tip drumstick in the 1950s to prolong the life of sticks. Wooden tips are usually the first part of a drumstick to

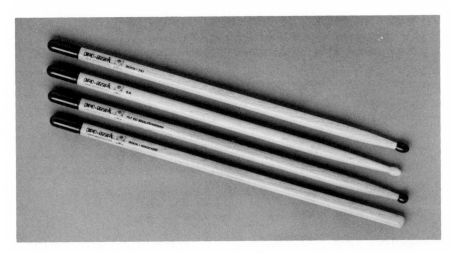

Pro-Mark ZX series Japanese oak drumsticks with nylon butt caps, (*top to bottom*) with acorn shape nylon tip, with wood tip, with round nylon tip, double-butted model. (*Courtesy of Pro-Mark Corp.*)

show wear. After the lacquer sealant wears off, they become soft and chipped, producing a mushy, indistinct sound on cymbals. When this happens, some drummers paint the wooden tips of their sticks with wood varnish or clear nail polish to extend their life. Nylon solves this problem by producing a clear, crisp, well defined cymbal sound for the life of the stick.

There is only a slight difference between the sound and feel of new, identically sized nylon or wood tip drumsticks. This difference is most noticeable when striking cymbals, where the higher density of the nylon produces a slightly brighter tonal quality. When striking drums, a blind-folded drummer probably would not know the difference between wood or nylon tips.

An interesting variation on the nylon tip idea is the Pro-Mark ZX series of oak drumsticks, featuring nylon butt caps for a brighter sound when striking with the butt end of the stick. Trueline has a series of nylon/wood tip hickory sticks that feature a nylon tip with the front end cut off. Exposing the wood at the front of the nylon tip and reducing the size of the tip is supposed to produce a sound closer to wood with the durability of nylon. The difference is subtle, but it is an interesting idea.

If you are unfamiliar with the brand of nylon tip sticks that you are thinking of buying, check to be sure that the tips are good quality material and securely fastened to the wood. Poor quality tips can split, shatter (if they are made of a hard plastic) or fly off the stick during use if they are

Trueline hickory drumsticks, showing Trueline Grip "bump" at point of grip.
(Courtesy of Trueline Drumstick Co.)

not firmly attached. Also, hard plastic tips (unlike nylon) produce a harsh sound on cymbals.

Drumstick sizing is confusing these days. At one time, most North American drumsticks were grouped into A, B or S series. The letter A indicated a relatively thin, light stick for "orchestral" or low-to-medium volume applications. The letter B stood for "band" series, somewhat thicker and heavier sticks for higher volume applications. The letter S meant "street" sticks, the largest, thickest and heaviest models, designed specifically for high volume, outdoor applications such as marching bands.

Models within each series were numbered like this: 1A, 2A, 3A, 4A, 5A, etc.; 1B, 2B, 3B, 4B, 5B, etc.; 1S, 2S, 3S, etc.

Although standardization of sizes between manufacturers could not be relied on, the general idea for A and B series was that model number 1 was the longest and thickest, with each successive model slightly shorter and or thinner. The S series reversed this process, with model 1S being the lightest stick and each successive model becoming heavier.

With the passage of time, unpopular models were dropped. Some manufacturers still use the number-and-letter designations on the remaining popular sizes, but the current trend is to name sticks for their intended application or for a well known drummer who uses that model.

If you play the same style of music at a consistent volume level all the time, you may be content with one favorite size of stick. Handling different styles and volume levels is easier if you know how to select appropriate stick sizes for each application.

The variety of available sizes and shapes gives many choices, but the lack of standardization requires some homework to find out what is available. Obtain catalogs from your favorite drumstick companies that show the dimensions of each model. Every drummer has a preference for certain stick dimensions.

Drumstick length varies from approximately 14¾" to 17½". Different drummers prefer different amounts of "reach" with their sticks. Length also has a subtle effect on volume. For the same amount of movement of the drummer's hands, the tip of a short stick will move through a relatively short arc, while the tip of a long stick will move through a longer arc. The longer the arc, the faster the tip is traveling when it strikes. Greater speed imparts more energy to the drumhead or cymbal, creating more volume. A tip traveling through a shorter arc strikes with less speed, producing less volume (assuming that the sticks are of equal thickness and different lengths). So it is easier to play softly with a short stick and loudly with a long stick, other factors being equal. Some manufacturers, such as Rimshot, offer otherwise traditional size models of sticks with slight additional length. This provides more reach and volume without changing to a larger overall stick.

Because it takes more time for the tip of a stick to move through a longer arc, greater length has a slightly negative effect on speed. It is a bit easier to play fast with a shorter stick, because the tip must travel less distance for each stroke. Also, a longer stick weighs more than a shorter stick of the same thickness, requiring more effort to manipulate it.

Shaft thickness varies from approximately 7⁄16" to 11⁄16". Greater thickness means more weight. While a thicker, heavier stick may cut your speed slightly by requiring more effort, it is an excellent choice for the heavy player for a couple of reasons. First, in a high volume situation, a heavy stick will do much of the work for you, producing a deep, solid tonal quality and more volume. Because of its additional weight, it does this with less effort than striking hard with a light stick. Second, a thicker drumstick can take more punishment than a thin stick without breaking. Drummers who break sticks frequently may be using a stick that is too thin for the volume or tonal quality they want, forcing them to over-play. The lighter player will probably find it easier to play at low volume using a thinner stick.

The dimensions of tip, neck and taper on a drumstick influence the sound it produces, its rebound characteristics and its durability. Because sticks usually break at the neck or the taper, durability can sometimes be adequately enhanced by increasing the thickness of these areas rather than choosing a stick with greater overall thickness. Several manufacturers offer sticks with thicker necks and more abrupt tapers than traditional models to withstand heavy playing. This extra weight at the forward end of the stick (compared to a thinner neck and taper) also changes the feel and balance point. The Regal Quantum series from Calato includes models that eliminate the neck of the stick for greater resistance to breakage. Several companies offer double butted models with no taper, neck or tip.

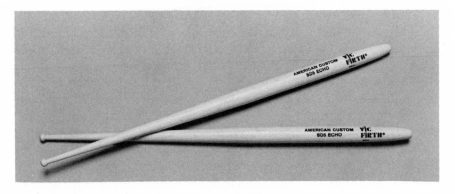

Vic Firth SD5 Echo model maple drumsticks. Notice the extremely long, thin taper. This stick is designed for very soft playing and creates a delicate sound on both drums and cymbals. *(Courtesy of Vic Firth, Inc.)*

These are the most extreme examples of drumsticks designed primarily for durability.

Large tips, thick necks and abrupt tapers make sticks rather rigid. Hefty sticks produce a full, deep tonal quality and more volume on drums. They also produce a loud, harsh tone on cymbals. Small tips, thin necks and long, gradual tapers make sticks more flexible. The thinner the neck and longer the taper, the less suitable they are for heavy playing. Sticks of this configuration produce less volume, more high overtones and a more delicate tonal quality on drums and especially on cymbals. One of the most extreme examples is the Vic Firth SD5 Echo model, originally designed for ultra-soft orchestral playing. Its long taper and small tip make it excellent for use in low volume situations and far too delicate for hard playing. The Regal Tip Silhouette model is a more traditional configuration of "pencil" stick, which is the term drummers often use for thin sticks designed for low volume playing.

Large sticks usually have large tips and smaller sticks usually have small tips, reinforcing the tonal characteristics produced by the overall stick design. Exceptions to the rule can create an interesting compromise. The Peter Erskine signature model stick from Vic Firth, for example has a relatively abrupt taper with a very small tip. This gives it a fairly rigid feel and good durability for its shaft thickness while the small tip produces a delicate sound on cymbals.

When playing a steady rhythm on a ride cymbal, you can influence its tonal quality to some degree by varying your angle of attack with the stick. Striking with the stick almost parallel to the surface of the cymbal produces a louder, harsher sound, while playing at a greater angle lightens the sound. Combining this technique with different sizes of sticks for different applications can create a wide spectrum of sound options. The same idea is true for hi-hat cymbals, with the harshest tone being achieved by striking the shaft of the stick across the edge of the top hi-hat cymbal.

The most important thing to consider regarding stick dimensions is whether the sticks feel right for you. Some sizes will work well but you will have trouble using others. Most drummers are fussy about the way a stick feels and reacts as they play. The only time you might ignore your instincts in this matter is when you are trying to correct a sound or breakage problem. Using a different size of stick that is more appropriate for the application may feel strange at first but you may be able to overcome this feeling if you give it time. Sometimes these problems can be corrected by switching to a model with only a slight difference in dimensions.

There are several unique drumstick designs and accessory products that can solve performance problems or add interesting effects to your playing. For instance, the Trueline Drum Stick Company has a series of Trueline Grip models that feature a bump (an enlargement of shaft diameter) at the point where the stick is gripped. This is intended to keep the stick from sliding out of your hand without the necessity of gripping it tightly. It also provides a point of increased leverage for drummers who use finger control technique. Some other manufacturers use grooves cut into the stick in the gripping area to improve grip.

Pro-Mark's Gerry Brown Double Header sticks have an identical taper, neck and tip at each end, making them useful for back-sticking and stick twirling applications. Vic Firth's Carmine Appice model has a traditional 5A wood tip at one end and a second, larger wooden tip carved at the butt end, giving better feel and definition than the usual butt when playing with the sticks reversed for more volume.

Vic Firth SD6 and SD12 Swizzle models are drumsticks with felt mallet heads on the butt ends. This is a useful feature for the drummer who must switch from sticks to mallets (or vice versa) without stopping. Mike Balter Mallets manufactures a series of Louis Bellson drumset mallets, most of which are actually combinations of sticks, brushes and mallets. They include a stick with a brush at the butt end, a stick with a mallet at the butt end, a brush with a mallet at the butt end, a stick with a wire brush at the same end as the tip and sticks with tambourine jingles attached to the shaft.

The Rota Tip Drum Stick Company offers the Flexi-tip stick. This is a nylon tip drumstick with two additional nylon tips on a flexible piece of plastic that is inserted through the stick at its shoulder. When you strike the stick against a drumhead or cymbal, the additional tips bounce against the surface, creating a multiple stroke effect.

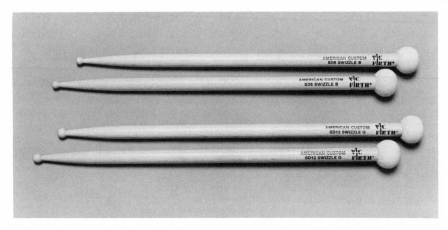

Vic Firth SD6 Swizzle B and SD12 Swizzle G drumsticks with hard felt mallet heads on the butt ends. The combination of stick and mallet allows you to get either sound without switching sticks. *(Courtesy of Vic Firth, Inc.)*

To prevent sticks from slipping out of the drummer's hands due to perspiration and to absorb some of the "stick shock" that drummers' hands receive during heavy playing, several companies sell gloves designed for drumming. They may also prevent the blisters or calluses that are a problem for some drummers. Wearing gloves while playing is an acquired taste. Some drummers find them very useful while others find playing with them awkward and uncomfortable.

An alternative is stick tape, such as Pro-Mark Stick Rapp. Wrapping the gripping area of the stick with this tape cushions the hand against shock and provides a better grip than a bare stick for sweaty hands. Another alternative is the Shock Grip available on some models of Aquarian drumsticks. These are flexible sleeves that fit permanently over the butt end of the stick, covering the gripping area.

Here is a simple test to perform every time a new pair of drumsticks is selected, regardless of their size or type:

1. Before you buy them, remove them from their package and inspect the grain of the wood. It should run along the length of the stick. Any stick with the grain running across it, especially near the thinner end, should be rejected; the stick could break easily at this point. For synthetic sticks, inspect the material for flaws that might be weak spots. For sticks with nylon tips, inspect the tip to see that it appears firmly attached to the stick.

2. Use a flat table or sales counter to roll the sticks back and forth. If they roll smoothly, they are straight. If they wobble as they roll, they are warped and should be rejected. Drummers call warped sticks "bananas"

because their curved shape resembles a banana in extreme cases. A badly warped stick feels very awkward to most drummers.

3. Strike each stick on a hard surface such as a table or sales counter. If a stick feels "mushy" rather than solid as you strike it and does not produce a clear tone, it may be cracked. Listen to the pitch produced by each stick and feel their weight. Assuming that you want a matched pair, both sticks should feel equally heavy and produce a similar pitch. The pitch test is not as definite because it can be influenced by your grip, the angle of the stroke and the amount of force used. Sticks cannot be guaranteed against breakage but they will last longer and perform better if they are in perfect shape when you buy them.

Ideally, a drumstick should wear out rather than break. Constant striking causes nicks and dents. Wood will chip and wear away anywhere the stick contacts a drum or cymbal. Even the synthetic materials eventually reach the limit of their strength and resilience. If you are buying good quality sticks and experiencing frequent breakage after minimal use, it indicates a mistake in your choice of stick size and or a problem in your technique. Check your sticks occasionally for signs of cracking, wear and warpage and replace them when necessary. The sharp end of a broken stick can pierce a drumhead, so discard sticks that are badly worn, chipped and ready to break.

Striking cymbals incorrectly is a common cause of stick breakage. Try to avoid stiking directly into the edge of a cymbal. This is hard on cymbals as well as sticks. Contacting the cymbal's edge with a downward stroke or a side to side downward sweep produces a great crash sound while prolonging stick and cymbal life. Alternately, try pulling the stick back as you strike instead of playing "through" the cymbal. Also, the use of a loose, relaxed grip allows a stick to dissipate some of the energy of the stroke. A tight, rigid grip forces the stick to absorb much of the energy, which accelerates wear.

A rimshot is executed by simultaneously striking the drumhead and the counterhoop with the same stick. If the neck or taper of the stick contacts the metal counterhoop, breakage is more likely. Practice striking rimshots with the shaft of the stick contacting the counterhoop instead.

Striking the drumhead heavily without allowing the stick to rebound and dissipate the vibration energy increases the likelihood of stick and or head breakage. Do not hold the stick against the head at the completion of each stroke. Allowing it to rebound after touching the head also produces a louder and more distinct tone.

Make note of the dimensions, material and any special features of the sticks you like. This can help you to choose alternatives when you need just a slight change in size or weight.

Regal Tip traditional wire brushes in four variations, *(left to right)* **non-retractable wooden grip, retractable metal grip, non-retractable rubber grip, retractable rubber grip.** *(Courtesy of Calato Manufacturing.)*

Brushes

Brushes are not as popular as they were a generation ago. The high volume of modern music made them impractical. More widespread use of amplification on acoustic drums and innovations in brush design have led to a resurgence in their use, however. Brush playing is audible again and many drummers are discovering the beautiful sound textures that brushes can create. A little time spent practicing with a pair of brushes will add a whole range of subtle effects to your technique.

There are several variations of wire brushes. All of them have a number of thin, metal wires protruding from a shaft that acts as a handle or gripping area. The shaft may be made of wood, plastic, metal or rubber-covered metal and either smooth finished or textured for a better grip.

Wire brushes are either retractable or non-retractable. Retractable brushes allow the wires to be telescoped into the shaft when not in use to prevent them from being bent or kinked. Some models require you to push the wires into the shaft and pull them out or flick them out with a jerk of

Regal Ed Thigpen model brushes, a plastic wire brush with a pliable plastic grip. *(Courtesy of Calato Manufacturing.)*

the wrist. Other designs are retracted by means of a wire loop protruding from the butt end of the shaft.

The wire loop or butt end of the shaft may be covered by a rubber cap or knob, making it possible to reverse the brush and play with the butt end when a harder sound is needed. If uncovered, the wire loop can produce interesting cymbal glissando effects if it is swept across the cymbal grooves.

Wire brushes are also categorized by their spread, meaning the width of the fan of wires when fully extended. Wide spread brushes create delicate sweeping effects on drumheads, while narrow spread brushes produce better slap sounds. Regal Tip retractable brushes have a patented adjustable-spread feature that allows you to extend the wires fully for a wide spread or retract them slightly for a narrow spread. Being able to lock the wires in an extended position avoids the problem of the wires creeping back into the shaft during use, a common design problem with some retractable brushes. When selecting brushes, watch for that and for loose construction that can cause rattles.

Bent wires are the usual indicator of a worn-out brush. A few bent wires can be clipped off close to the shaft but when a significant number of wires are tangled or heading in different directions, it is time to buy a new pair of brushes. The choice between styles is largely a matter of personal preference. Non-retractable wire brushes must be stored more carefully than retractable ones to prolong the straightness of the wires. Wood, plastic, metal or rubber-covered handles affect the weight, feel and balance of brushes. Choose the ones that feel and react best for your playing style.

Vic Firth jazz rakes and rock rakes, retractable plastic wire brushes. Jazz rakes have thinner plastic strands for lighter playing. Rock rakes have thicker plastic strands for heavier, louder playing. *(Courtesy of Vic Firth, Inc.)*

The innovations in brush design that I mentioned earlier involve the use of plastic strands rather than metal wires. Plastic, being thicker and stiffer than the metal wires, produces a harsher sound and more volume. Plastic brushes also withstand more energetic playing without developing permanent kinks in the strands. Brushes made from this material have a sound quality somewhere between that of a wire brush and a drumstick. The use of thicker or thinner plastic strands modifies the sound for different applications and volume requirements. Examples of this are Calato's Blasticks, Vic Firth's Rock Rakes and Latin Percussion's Heavy brushes, which are designed for a louder sound. Calato's Ed Thigpen model brushes, Vic Firth's Jazz Rakes, Latin Percussion's Light brushes and Pro-Mark's nylon brushes are designed for a softer plastic brush sound. Each of these examples has its own sound and feel, some of them distinctly different. Experimentation is worthwhile to find the one that sounds and feels best for the application you have in mind.

Most plastic brushes eventually fray at the ends of the strands, making their sound less distinct and necessitating replacement. A new pair sounds clearer and sharper. Before you throw away the old pair, however, try this tip. Melt the frayed ends of each plastic strand with a match or lighter. The resulting blob of hard plastic at the end of each strand produces an even sharper sound on drums or cymbals than an ordinary plastic brush, giving you another sound option.

Another innovation in "brush" technology is Pro-Mark's Multi-Rods. Multi-Rods consist of birch dowels, 1/8" diameter x 16" long banded together in bunches of 19. Being wood, they produce a sound closer in tonal quality to a drumstick than a brush but their unique construction

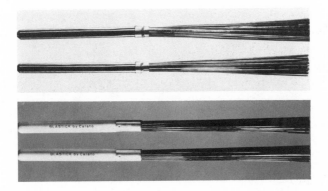

Top and middle: Calato Blasticks, non-retractable plastic wire brushes with thick plastic strands for loud playing. Notice the choice of wooden or plastic grips. *(Courtesy of Calato Manufacturing.) Bottom:* Pro-Mark Rods, bundles of thin birch rods that create a sound somewhere between a brush and a stick. *(Courtesy of Pro-Mark Corp.)*

gives their sound more spread than a solid drumstick. They also have a natural rebound or bounce to their feel that a brush does not have.

Mallets

A mallet is basically a drumstick with a specialized head in place of the usual drumstick tip. The shafts of most mallets suitable for drumset use are made of wood, although metal and synthetic materials are sometimes used. The shaft and mallet head may be of one piece construction (like the wooden headed mallets designed for timpani use) but more often, the mallet head is made of a different material glued or screwed onto the shaft.

Mallets are used on a drumset to get a different tonal quality from the drums and cymbals than is normally produced by sticks or brushes. The tonal quality produced by a specific mallet is determined primarily by the material used for the mallet head. The material, thickness and taper of shaft also affect the sound to a small extent. There is a wide variety of sound choices available, from hard mallet head materials like brass or nylon to increasingly softer mallet heads of rubber, yarn or cord-wound materials and felt or lambswool-covered felt. Every drummer should experiment with various mallets to discover the dramatic effects they can produce, especially on toms and cymbals.

Calato Saul Goodman timpani mallets and snare drumsticks, showing some of the variations in mallet head shapes and sizes. Although not obvious in a photograph, the felt heads are also varying degrees of hardness or softness. *(Courtesy of Calato Manufacturing.)*

Some drumstick manufacturers make a relatively small selection of felt mallets specifically for drumset use. A wider variety of mallet head materials and degrees of hardness or softness can be found by trying the mallets designed for timpani or keyboard percussion instruments. These are also made by drumstick companies and by specialty mallet manufacturers. Some are not designed to withstand rough use and should be treated carefully.

Top quality mallets cost more than drumsticks but will last for many years with reasonable care. When selecting mallets, look for securely fastened heads that will not fly off the shaft during use. If you are a particularly heavy player, you will need the durability of mallets designed for heavy duty marching band and drum corps use. Check your mallets regularly for loose or worn heads and cracked or warped shafts, replacing them when necessary.

Beaters

Bass drum foot pedal beaters are specially designed mallets with a metal shaft that fits into the foot pedal. Some beater shafts have a

Drum Workshop bass drum foot pedal showing reversible felt or hard plastic beater head. *(Courtesy of Drum Workshop.)*

flattened side on the end that fits into the pedal to provide more solid attachment and prevent the shaft from rotating as it is played. Standard beater shafts are approximately one-quarter inch thick. Most are made from hardened steel to prevent bending. Extremely heavy players may find the extra-thick shafts offered on such pedals as the Calato Regal Tip model useful. Thick beater shafts will only fit the pedals designed to receive them.

Standard beater shaft lengths may not be adequate to reach the center of large diameter bass drums. If you encounter this problem, you can buy beaters with extra-long shafts from accessory companies. Although most bass drum pedals are supplied with hard felt beaters as original equipment, this material is not the only choice for beater heads. Optional materials are offered by some pedal manufacturers and other companies such as Danmar Percussion Products and Pro-Mark.

The three traditional materials used for beater heads are lambswool-covered felt, hard felt and wood. The soft surface of lambswool produces the softest attack sound and is good for low volume applications. Hard felt produces a medium intensity attack sound and is good for all around playing, which explains its use as original equipment on most pedals. Wood produces a strong attack sound and is good for high volume applications. If your volume requirements or the acoustics of the rooms in which you

Sonor bass drum multi-beater with interchangeable striking surfaces of wood, felt, rubber and acrylic. *(Courtesy of Korg U.S.A.)*

perform vary, you should have both hard felt and wood beaters available. Always carry a selection of beaters for different tonal requirements, room acoustics and volume requirements.

Other materials sometimes used are leather-covered felt (which gives an attack sound sharper than felt but softer than wood) and various hard synthetics that sound similar to wood. Combination beaters are available with two different striking surfaces on the same beater head. One example is the hard plastic beater reversing to felt that is supplied with some Drum Workshop pedals. Sonor offers their SCH27 Multi-beater, a unique design with four interchangeable striking heads (felt, wood and two different synthetics). You choose any two and put them together to make a reversible beater. The other two are small enough to fit in a pocket in your stick bag.

As well as differences in material, the standard rounded shape of beater heads is sometimes varied. Square beaters (such as Pro-Mark's Thumpers) or beaters with flattened striking surfaces are the most common variations. A square or flattened beater spreads the striking force over a larger area, slightly reducing bass drum batter head wear. However, they must be adjusted precisely so that the edge of the flattened area does not strike the head or they will actually increase batter head wear. This sometimes involves bending the beater shaft to align the flat surface with the head. If adjusted correctly, a flat surface beater also tends to produce a slightly deeper, more solid tonal quality than a round headed beater in the same way that heavier drumsticks affect the sound of other drums. This option is worth trying but has less effect than head type, tuning and muffling on the sound of your bass drum.

There are two things to check regularly on your bass drum beater. First, check the way the beater head is attached to the shaft to be certain that it is not working loose. Second, check the condition of the beater head material. Lambswool wears away after long use. Felt wears and deforms under heavy-footed playing. Wood occasionally chips or splits after hard use. Replace your beater if any of these conditions develop. If you use a quality felt beater and it deforms badly after minimal use, you are over-playing it and you should switch to a wood or hard synthetic beater.

Cymbals

It is the sound of cymbals combined with the sound of drums that creates the characteristic drumset sound. Many drummers do not realize that they strike their cymbals far more often than they strike their drums while playing most forms of popular music. Cymbals are an extremely important part of a drumset and their selection, care and use should reflect this importance.

Materials and Construction

Cymbals are far more complex instruments than they appear to be. In order to understand them, a drummer must first be familiar with the terminology used to describe the parts of a cymbal. The raised portion in the center is called the "cup" or "bell." Striking a cymbal here produces a brighter, more piercing tone than striking the main body of the cymbal. In the middle of the bell is the mounting hole that allows you to mount the cymbal on a stand. The area from the bell to the edge is called the "bow" or "taper." From the point of view of intended use, this is also called the "ride area" because striking here produces the best effect for "riding" (playing a steady rhythm) on the cymbal. The first couple of inches in from the edge is the "crash area." Striking here gives the best crash effect.

Most professional quality cymbals are made from bronze, which is a combination of copper, tin and trace metals. The two most common types of bronze used are usually called B20 and B8, the numbers referring to the percentage of tin that is blended with the copper. Cymbals can be made from other metals. For instance, Sabian uses a nickel-silver alloy for their Carmine Appice Signature series Chinese cymbal. Ace Products has a series of brass cymbals in addition to bronze in their Camber

Left: Sabian Carmine Appice Signature Series Chinese cymbals, made from nickel-silver alloy. *(Courtesy of Sabian.) Right:* Camber Germany Savage series crash/ride cymbal, showing unlathed surface with hammering marks. *(Courtesy of Ace Products.)*

Germany line. Paiste has developed a different, patented bronze alloy that is used in their Paiste series (sometimes referred to as the Paiste Signature series).

Some cymbals are manufactured by casting their source metal into ingots that are heated and rolled several times to a precise thickness. By passing the metal through rollers in a different direction each time, it develops a complex, interwoven grain structure. Sabian, Zildjian and some other manufacturers perform these stages of manufacture for most of their cymbals in their own factories. Other companies, such as Paiste, obtain the resulting metal from a metal fabricating company.

Non-cast cymbals, made from metal with a grain structure running in only one direction, are also available. This less complex grain structure tends to produce a more focused sound with a narrower range of overtones than a cast cymbal. Some cymbal manufacturers offer different lines of cast and non-cast cymbals. You can find examples of good and bad sounding cymbals of both types. Your choice between cast and non-cast cymbals should be guided by your personal preference in sound. The following manufacturing steps apply to both types.

When the metal reaches the proper thickness, the bell is pressed in and the cymbal is hammered into shape by hand or by machine. The edge is trimmed to create the cymbal's finished diameter and metal is removed from each side of the cymbal by means of a lathe. This creates the exact thickness desired and produces grooves in the surface of the cymbal.

Some brands of cymbals have a reputation for consistency of sound between identical examples while other brands are noted for individuality

Above: Paiste (signature) series cymbals, showing imprinted descriptions of sound, function and size. *(Courtesy of Paiste America.) Below:* Some of the many types of Zildjian cymbals. *(Courtesy of Zildjian.)*

of sound. For instance, two identical models of Paiste cymbals would probably be very similar in sound while two identical models of Zildjian cymbals could sound noticeably different. Camber Germany and Meinl are other manufacturers known for consistency of sound, while Sabian, Ufip and Istanbul are other examples of cymbals noted for variance of sound.

There are drummers who appreciate being able to replace a broken or lost cymbal with an identical model, secure in the knowledge that its sound will closely resemble the old cymbal. It also simplifies the process of cymbal selection when you do not have to try several identical cymbals to find the "right" one. Other drummers prefer the individuality of sound provided by less consistent cymbals, feeling that it gives them more opportunity for personal expression of their musical taste. The choice is one of personal preference.

Types and Features

The history of cymbals produced for drumset use is a story of increasing specialization. Although it is possible to use almost any cymbal in any application, years of experimentation by cymbal manufacturers has led to the development of specialized cymbals for specific functions. You will get better results by choosing a cymbal designed for your intended purpose.

Cymbals commonly used on the drumset can be divided into four basic categories based on application:

ride cymbals	hi-hat cymbals
crash cymbals	special-effects cymbals

Within these categories there are several variations. Ride cymbals are used primarily to play steady rhythms and keep time. Crash cymbals are used primarily to accent or punctuate the music. Hi-hat cymbals are played in pairs against each other and with sticks, primarily for steady rhythms and time keeping. Special-effects cymbals are used for crash or ride work in situations where a distinctly different sound is desired.

In addition to differences in material and methods of construction, cymbals vary by size, weight, curvature of bow, size of bell and surface finish. Different combinations of these variables emphasize certain sound characteristics, making a cymbal most suitable for a specific application. If you understand how each variable affects sound, you will have an easier time finding the cymbals you want.

The appearance of a cymbal can be used to create visual impact. Some surface finishes are primarily cosmetic while others have a noticeable effect

Camber Germany 300 series hi-hat cymbals, an example of brass cymbals. *(Courtesy of Ace Products.)*

on sound. Although the effect can be enhanced or moderated by other factors, some generalizations can be made. Usually, the smoother the surface of a given cymbal, the more definition and fewer overtones it has. The lathe grooves on a regularly finished cymbal tend to break up the vibrations as they travel from the edge to the bell and back, creating a shimmering sound that is comprised of overtones. The smoothing of these lathe grooves that occurs when the cymbal is polished or buffed to give it a brilliant, reflective finish creates less interference for the passage of the vibrations over the surface of the cymbal. A brilliant finish gives a cymbal a slightly brighter edge to its sound when compared to an identical cymbal with a regular, lathed finish. Zildjian says that this adds "warmth" to the sound of the cymbal while Sabian indicates that it adds a "cutting edge" to the sound. This is an example of the subjective terminology that drummers use to describe sounds, making it necessary for you to hear and decide for yourself.

Some cymbals are manufactured with no lathe grooves at all, giving them an even brighter, somewhat raw sound and a more piercing tonal quality that is useful for loud volume performance situations. Some of these, such as the Zildjian Z series, feature unique hammering patterns in the shape of stars and other geometric figures that are supposed to influence the sound. Sabian's Jack DeJohnette Signature series cymbals are not lathed or hammered, giving them a brown, unfinished appearance and a particularly dry sound with very little overtone. Other examples of un-lathed cymbals are the Camber Germany Savage series, the Sabian Leopard series and the Paiste Rude series.

Examples of strictly cosmetic finishes are Zildjian's Platinum and Paiste's Colorsound series. The Platinum cymbals are regular bronze cymbals electroplated with silver-colored metal. Colorsound cymbals are normal bronze cymbals with a surface coating available in several colors. In each case, the finish is supposed to have no noticeable effect on the sound.

A word about the durability of various surface finishes is important. The highly polished finish created by buffing a cymbal is actually easier to clean than a regular lathed finish because it is smoother, but this smoother finish also shows scratches more readily. Plated finishes, like Zildjian's Platinum series, are supposed to be no less durable than an unplated cymbal. Early examples suffered from peeling of the plating but this has apparently been corrected. The colored coatings applied to cymbals such as Paiste's Colorsound series are less durable, requiring careful handling and packing to avoid scratching the surface coating.

The size of a cymbal is the measurement of its diameter (given in inches in this book). They range in size from 8″ to 24″, generally in increments of one inch, with occasional exceptions outside this range. The larger the cymbal, the greater its volume. A large cymbal can be played softly, but it will react more fully at higher volume levels. Any cymbal has a maximum potential volume, beyond which it produces distortion rather than musical sound and risks breakage. Heavy players who experience frequent cymbal breakage can often eliminate this problem and produce the volume they need by using larger cymbals rather than over-playing smaller ones.

Large cymbals respond more slowly and sustain longer than small cymbals. For this reason as well as volume requirements, softer players ofter prefer slightly smaller cymbals for their quicker response and shorter sustain.

Response and sustain characteristics are also affected by a cymbal's weight. Weight in any given size of cymbal is determined by its thickness. The following are typical examples of the sort of terminology used by cymbal manufacturers to describe weight/thickness, from thinnest/lightest to thickest/heaviest:

paper thin
thin
medium thin
medium
medium heavy
heavy
extra-heavy

In some cases, more application-oriented terms are used, such as Jazz Ride for a lightweight ride cymbal or Rock Crash for a heavy crash cymbal. Paiste has taken this one step further with their Paiste (signature) series by using a chart to show the relationship in sound between the various choices of ride, crash or hi-hat cymbals and naming each variation for its tonal characteristics rather than its weight/thickness.

Increased weight affects response and sustain similarly to increased size. So a thin cymbal, when crashed, attains its maximum rate of vibration quickly and the sound dies out quickly. A thick cymbal, when crashed, attains its maximum rate of vibration slowly and the sound takes a long time to die out. Alternative terms for "response" and "sustain" are "attack" and "decay," respectively.

The weight/thickness of a cymbal also affects its pitch. As with drums, cymbals produce a fundamental pitch and a range of overtones, allowing them to blend harmoniously with whatever note or chord other musicians are playing. The thicker the cymbal, the higher the pitch. The thinner the cymbal, the lower the pitch. It should be noted here that size has an effect on pitch, too, in relation to weight. Two cymbals of the same thickness but different sizes will be pitched differently. The smaller cymbal will have a higher pitch than the larger cymbal of the same weight.

The degree of curvature in the bow of a cymbal from the bell to the edge also influences pitch and proportion of overtones in the sound. Flatter curvature produces lower pitch and more overtones. More pronounced curvature produces higher pitch and fewer overtones.

The height and diameter of the bell also influences the relative presence of overtones in the sound of the cymbal. Large bells produce more overtones, quicken the attack and lengthen the decay. Progressively smaller bells produce correspondingly fewer overtones, giving good definition to each stroke. The complete absence of a bell makes a cymbal incapable of building much overtone and gives maximum definition to each stroke.

Each variable of cymbal design has an effect on the contribution of every other variable to the resulting sound. The number of possible permutations of these factors accounts for the almost overwhelming list of cymbal choices available. When you divide cymbals into the categories of intended use mentioned earlier, the choice becomes clearer and less daunting because certain characteristics are most appropriate for specific uses. For instance, ride cymbals, used for time keeping and steady rhythms, must have minimal overtone buildup and clear stroke definition. In contrast to this, crash cymbals must have quicker response, full overtone sound and reasonably quick decay to punctuate dramatically and not cloud the music following the accent.

Left: Sabian HH Classic ride cymbal. *Right:* Sabian cymbals. Note small diameter "bell" cymbal *(top right)* and upturned edge of Chinese cymbal *(top left).* *(Courtesy of Sabian.)*

Planning Your Set-Up

Cymbal manufacturers design their cymbals for such basic applications and label them so that a knowledgeable drummer can pick the correct one for the intended use. By the mid–1960s, most cymbals were labeled as ride, crash, hi-hat, etc. Weight/thickness terminology was also used and a range of sizes was available in each category. As the years passed, terms such as the previously mentioned Jazz Ride and Rock Crash became common. There is now a complete series of cymbals designed for different playing styles or musical applications. Without suggesting a direct comparison between the products of various manufacturers, it is possible to give some simplified examples of this.

Drummers in extremely high volume situations require large, heavy cymbals that produce adequate volume and resist breakage during hard use. They also require a bright, piercing tonal quality capable of projecting to the audience through a high ambient noise level. The heavy, unlathed cymbals in the Zildjian Z series, the Sabian Leopard series and the Paiste Rude series are all designed to accomplish this more efficiently than the other series of cymbals in their respective lines.

At the opposite end of the scale, drummers in low volume performance situations require smaller, lighter cymbals with sensitive response and more delicate tone. Too much cutting edge would overpower the band and be unsuitable. The Zildjian K series, some of the Sabian HH series and the Paiste 602 series are choices worth considering for this application. Although substantially different from each other, each is an example of cymbal design well suited to low volume use.

It is possible to use the same cymbals to play quiet jazz in a small room or loud rock at an outdoor stadium, but you will get better results, especially if your cymbals are not amplified, by making different choices for different circumstances. If you play a wide variety of music and cannot afford separate sets of cymbals for different styles and volume levels, you will have to compromise in your selection to cover as many bases as possible with relatively few cymbals.

For years, most drummers played any style of music with two ride/ crash cymbals and a pair of hi-hat cymbals. Now, with more choice and increased specialization of cymbal sounds, it is common to see drummers surrounded by elaborate cymbal set-ups. Any cymbal set-up, from the most basic to the most elaborate, should provide you with different sound choices for different musical needs. Cymbals should be chosen to blend harmoniously if they are struck simultaneously. Without ignoring that requirement, each cymbal must be sufficiently different in sound characteristics to add a distinct tonal color to the drumset. Sound variety within a harmonious range is the key. The most common error drummers make is to use several crash cymbals that sound alike. Unless the cymbals are there purely for decoration, this is a waste of money.

A basic cymbal set-up for any type of popular music includes a ride cymbal, a crash cymbal and a pair of hi-hat cymbals. Ride cymbals range in size from 16" to 24". Crash cymbals range in size from 8" to 20". Hi-hat cymbals range in size from 10" to 16". With so many different styles of music, volume levels and personal tastes to consider, it is impossible to recommend the right cymbal set-up for every drummer. A catalog from your favorite cymbal manufacturer will show you what is available.

Lighter players who use light sticks should consider smaller, lighter cymbals that respond well at low volume. Heavy players who use heavy sticks should consider larger, heavier cymbals that produce more volume and withstand heavy playing with less likelihood of cracking. Just like a drum, it is the higher pitched portion of a cymbal's sound that provides the cutting power to project through loud music. In situations where no cymbal amplification is used, higher pitched cymbals are perceived as louder than lower pitched cymbals.

If you plan to add to this basic set-up later, make your initial choices with that in mind. For instance, most drummers add a second crash cymbal. If one crash cymbal must handle all the work, it should be a compromise size and weight that will produce both the strong and delicate crash effects you will need. If you plan to use two crash cymbals, one can be larger and heaver to do a better job on strong crashes, while the other can be smaller and or lighter to do a better job on softer, more subtle crashes. To be sure that they do not sound the same, a good rule of thumb is to separate these two cymbals by at least two inches in size and one or two increments of weight, for example: 18" medium crash and 16" thin crash.

Splash cymbals, ranging in size from 8" to 12" are the smallest, lightest crash cymbals in any series and make an interesting choice if you want a third crash cymbal. Again, this should be taken into account when making your initial selection so that your smaller crash cymbal will be separated from the pitch and tonal quality of the splash cymbal by at least a couple of inches and one or two weight increments.

Special-effects cymbals should be considered only after you have equipped yourself with the basics, since they are less versatile. Many special-effects cymbals are variations of "Chinese" cymbals, with upturned edges and various bell shapes that create distinctive tonal qualities. They are known variously as Chinese, Swish and Pang cymbals, each variation having its own sound. Years ago, some jazz drummers used Chinese cymbals as ride cymbals. These days, they are used most often for their explosive crash effects. In some musical situations they are very effective but in others they are unsuitable.

Other variations in design that fall into the special-effects category include Paiste's Sound Creation series. Sabian offers their Sound Control series, with flanged edges (flattened, rather than upturned like a Chinese cymbal) that shorten their decay and limit overtones. Sabian's Rocktagons are octagonal shaped crash cymbals with a distinctive, dissonant tonal quality created by their odd shape. When you strike a cymbal, the vibrations travel back and forth between the edge and the bell. The distance between edge and bell is constant on a round cymbal, creating similar frequencies of sound waves all around the edge. The distance between edge and bell on a Rocktagon varies from longer at the "corners" to shorter at the mid-point of each flat section. The resulting unmatched frequencies that are generated produce the Rocktagon's jarring sound.

Several manufacturers offer special-effect cymbals that consist primarily of a thick bell. These small diameter cymbals are designed to produce a loud, cutting bell sound with little or no overtone. Gongs of many sizes and types are also available. They have become popular with some rock and jazz drummers for their dramatic sound.

While not exactly cymbals, Remo Spoxe are special-effect items that produce a bell-like sound and are sometimes used in conjunction with cymbals. They are metal castings in various diameters, originally developed as part of Remo's RotoToms.

One option that is not seen often is the use of rivets in a cymbal. Many cymbals can be ordered from the manufacturer with rivets installed in holes drilled near the edge. The buzzing or sizzling effect created by the vibrating rivets when the cymbal is struck gives us the term "sizzle" cymbal. Sizzle cymbals were quite common at one time but higher volume levels reduced their popularity. A heavy player can knock the rivets out of a cymbal. The sizzling effect of the rivets prolongs the sustain and adds an interesting tonal quality that is most effective for lighter players at lower volume levels.

Rivets can be added to any cymbal but their installation requires knowledge and care to avoid damaging the cymbal. Proper cymbal rivets are available from many cymbal companies. If you wish to install them, the holes should be

Graduated sizes of Remo Spoxe mounted on boom stand for a "bell tree" effect. *(Courtesy of Remo, Inc.)*

drilled within ½" to 1" of the cymbal's edge. Too many rivets can dampen the sound of a cymbal rather than prolonging its sustain. The optimum number of rivets varies, depending on the size and weight of the cymbal. The following suggestions can be used as a basis for experimentation:

16" cymbal - 2 to 3 rivets   20" cymbal - 4 to 6 rivets
18" cymbal - 3 to 4 rivets   22" cymbal - 6 to 8 rivets

If you wish to try this effect to see if you like it before drilling a cymbal, there are accessory devices, such as the Pro-Mark Rattler, that vibrate against a cymbal and imitate the sound of rivets. If you want the sound of a sizzle cymbal only occasionally, the Rattler can be carried in your stick bag or trap case, adding to the versatility of a cymbal without making any permanent alterations to it.

Testing and Selecting Cymbals

Go to your local music store prepared to do a thorough test. Finding the correct cymbal is usually a process of elimination, trying many cymbals and rejecting the ones you do not like. Take your time and rest your ears occasionally if you become confused by all the different sounds.

If you are selecting one or more cymbals to add to your existing set-up, bring your cymbals with you to the store. Set them up on a drumset with one or more stands left empty for the new cymbals you are testing. You need to know how a new cymbal sounds with your old ones to avoid duplicating a sound and to be sure that their sounds blend nicely. If you are starting from scratch and selecting a complete cymbal set-up, start with all the cymbal stands empty. Bring a pair of drumsticks of the type you expect to use. Different drumsticks influence the sound of cymbals. If you use different sticks, brushes and mallets for different applications, bring your stick bag and try several pairs on each cymbal.

Pro-Mark Rattler, a chain device used to simulate the sound of a rivetted sizzle cymbal. *(Courtesy of Pro-Mark Corp.)*

A salesperson can help you by playing a cymbal while you stand across the room and listen. Remember that cymbals, like drums, sound differently up close to the drummer and out in the audience. Avoid any music store where you are discouraged from testing cymbals thoroughly before buying them.

Test one type of cymbal at a time. For instance, select a few sizes and weights of ride cymbals that might suit your musical style and volume requirements. When you have found the right one, try the hi-hat cymbals or crash cymbals. Many stores have display stands where you can do the initial testing to find the sizes and weights you wish to try out on a drumset. Do not try a cymbal by striking it while it is balanced on your finger. Your finger will muffle it unnaturally, giving you a false impression of the sound. If it is impossible to set up the cymbals on a drumset, put them on cymbal stands side by side. Set them all horizontally at the same height. Remember that hard or carpeted floor surfaces make a difference in the sound of drums and cymbals. Eliminate as many variables as possible to get a valid comparison.

Certain brands of cymbals will have much consistency in sound between identical models while other brands will vary noticeably in sound between identical models. Even within a manufacturer's line, there may be different series of cymbals with consistent or inconsistent sound characteristics. Trying a few identical models from a specific series of cymbals can point out these characteristics and a knowledgeable salesperson can save you some time by explaining what to expect in consistency among the brands of cymbals sold at the store.

In general, try to select cymbals with enough reserve power so that you will not be playing them at their maximum volume all the time. This minimizes the danger of over-playing, which can lead to broken cymbals. Do not choose cymbals designed for much louder volume levels than you require, however, or they will not respond properly at your desired volume.

To test a ride cymbal, play a steady rhythm on it between the edge and the bell. Move your stick around to hear how the cymbal sounds when struck in different areas. Play lightly, then "dig in" and play heavily. Listen to the pitch. Vary the angle of your stick (relative to the surface of the cymbal) from almost parallel to a much greater angle. A good ride cymbal should have clear definition of each stroke and should not build up so many overtones under hard playing that they obscure the stick definition. If you can crash on the edge of a ride cymbal and then play a steady rhythm on it, hearing each stroke through the sound of the crash, it has good definition. If not, the overtone buildup will obliterate your ride rhythm when you play heavily. Small-bell and flat-top ride cymbals are designed to give very clear definition but their bell sound (when they have bells) may not be bright enough for loud situations. Most ride cymbals are too heavy to produce a good crash sound.

Play the bell of the ride cymbal, first with the tip and then with the shoulder of the stick. You should get a clear, piercing tone, especially with the shoulder of the stick. Generally, the larger the bell, the louder and brighter the bell sound. The complete lack of a bell is one of the disadvantages of flat ride cymbals, making them less versatile. If you use a flat ride and need a bell sound, be certain that one of your other cymbals has a suitable sounding bell.

To test a crash cymbal, strike its edge with a side-to-side downward sweeping motion. Striking straight into the edge shortens the life of both cymbals and drumsticks. Strike it several times with varying levels of impact as you would when performing. Do not just tap it lightly. Listen to the pitch of the cymbal, how quickly it responds and how long the sound takes to die out. Using your knowledge of how each design factor affects sound, try larger, smaller, thicker or thinner cymbals to find the sound you want.

To test hi-hat cymbals, listen for a clear, well-defined "chick" sound when you operate the hi-hat pedal. To prevent air from becoming trapped between the cymbals and muffling the chick sound, some bottom hi-hat cymbals have rippled edges or holes drilled in them or sections cut from their edge. Try adjusting the tilting device for the bottom cymbal on the hi-hat stand to see how this affects the sound.

Factory matched pairs of hi-hat cymbals should sound harmonious when struck simultaneously. With the cymbals apart, try this and listen for any discordant overtones. The bottom cymbal is usually heavier than the top cymbal (and consequently higher pitched) to help produce a crisp chick sound. Mixing different types of top and bottom hi-hat cymbals to achieve certain sound qualities has become popular. Factory selected mixed pairs are available or you can select your own. Unless you are very experienced and know just what you want, the factory selected pairs are probably the best options.

Play the top cymbal with a stick, listening to the sound when the cymbals are completely closed, partially open and fully open. The closed sound should be clear and well-defined at your chosen volume level. Try both the tip of the stick on the top cymbal and the shoulder of the stick on the edge of the top cymbal for different effects. With the cymbals partially open but still touching, you should get a good sizzle sound. If the pitch or tonal quality of the top cymbal does not please you when the cymbals are fully open, you should experiment with pairs that are larger/thicker or smaller/thinner to find the ones that respond as you like.

To test special-effects cymbals, use the same procedure as for crash cymbals. The upturned edge of a Chinese cymbal is particularly hard on drumsticks. Many drummers mount this type of cymbal upside down, so they can strike it on the underside at the point where the edge begins to turn up. This also influences its sound, so you should experiment with right side up mounting as well to find different ride and crash effects.

If you need a complete set of cymbals and you find the preceding procedure a bit too complex, there is a simple solution to finding well-matched cymbals. Some manufacturers, such as Camber Germany and Sabian, offer factory-matched sets of cymbals in various price ranges. Most drummers buy factory-matched pairs of hi-hat cymbals and this is a logical extension of the idea. Most sets include a ride cymbal, a crash cymbal and a pair of hi-hat cymbals (you can add to this selection when you need more cymbal sounds). You will still have to listen to the set to be sure it is appropriate for your needs, but the process of selecting cymbals that sound good together has been done for you.

Care Tips

In order to mount Chinese cymbals upside down at a playable angle, many drummers tighten them firmly onto the stand. This muffles the cymbal, reducing its volume and sustain. A tightly mounted cymbal cannot vibrate freely when struck to dissipate the energy of the stroke. This leads to stress cracking at the edge or mounting hole, a major cause of breakage for all cymbals. If the cymbal must be held firmly at a particular angle, try using a Cymbal Spring made by Aquarian Accessories. This spring mount holds the cymbal in position but allows it to move when struck to help prevent cracking.

Until volume levels in popular music began to rise significantly, cracking a cymbal was considered unusual. Some heavy players now break so many cymbals that they regard them as replaceable, almost disposable items, like drumsticks or drumheads. Much of this breakage is avoidable, being due to improper cymbal selection, incorrect striking technique and tight mounting of cymbals. Just like Chinese cymbals, your ride and crash cymbals must be able to vibrate freely when struck. Tight mounting chokes a cymbal's resonance and reduces its volume, leading you to strike it harder. This also applies to the top hi-hat cymbal which should be able to move freely in the hi-hat clutch.

Another thing that muffles the resonance of a ride or crash cymbal is mounting it at an extreme angle. An angled cymbal presses against its mounting hardware, trying to regain a horizontal position. The greater the angle, the greater the temptation to tighten it on the stand to retain its angle. Always mount cymbals as close as possible to a horizontal position. This puts the least stress on the cymbal and creates the loudest, fullest, most resonant sound. When spatial limitations prevent this and you must use an extreme mounting angle, Aquarian Cymbal Springs can be used on ride and crash cymbals to maintain the mounting angle while allowing the cymbal to dissipate vibration when struck.

Another device designed specifically to keep ride cymbals from swaying when struck is the Cym-Set from the Corder Drum Company. It is a large, flexible, convex plastic washer that provides support to the underside of the cymbal's bell without noticeably muffling its sound. It makes overtightening unnecessary and flexes when the cymbal is struck solidly, but it should only be used for ride cymbals.

At the point where the cymbal touches the stand, metal to metal contact must be avoided. Most cymbal stands are made of chrome-plated steel, which is much harder than cymbal bronze. Rubbing against the stand will wear away metal from the cymbal, enlarging its mounting hole. Metal to metal contact also adversely affects the sound of a cymbal. Cymbals should rest loosely on a felt or rubber washer with plastic or rubber tubing covering the rod that passes through the mounting hole. The thickness and diameter of the felt washer under a cymbal can slightly affect its resonance. The more soft material in contact with the cymbal, the more muffling effect it produces. For this reason, you will probably rarely use a second felt washer on top of the cymbal. It is only needed to prevent the cymbal from contacting the wing nut at the top of the tilter and can often be dispensed with when a cymbal is mounted close to horizontal.

A bottom hi-hat cymbal should rest on a felt washer with a rubber or plastic tube protecting it from contact with the pull rod that passes through its mounting hole. Most hi-hat stands have a tilting device for the bottom cymbal to improve the contact between cymbals and to prevent air-lock between them.

A top hi-hat cymbal should be loosely sandwiched between two felt washers. The design of the hi-hat clutch that holds the top cymbal makes some intermittent metal to metal contact between the cymbal and the clutch inevitable.

Avoid dropping cymbals and protect them from nicks and scratches that can develop into cracks by storing and transporting them in some kind of case or cover. If possible, prevent the cymbals from scratching each other in the case by separating them in plastic or cloth bags or by putting plastic, fabric or other insulating material between them. This is particularly important for colored cymbals with their delicate surface coatings. The rivets in sizzle cymbals will scratch other cymbals in the case badly if they are not separated in this way. Regardless of your stick size or how heavily you play, cymbals, like drumheads, last longer if you play "off" their surface rather than into it. Glancing strokes are better than direct ones.

Cleaning

Some cymbals come from the factory with a wax-like coating to prevent tarnish. This coating eventually wears off with use and repeated cleaning. Similar tarnish protection can be achieved (or renewed) by applying a very light coating of spray-type furniture wax. Too much wax will muffle the sound of the cymbal, so apply it quite sparingly and buff off the excess with a soft cloth in the direction of the grooves on the cymbal's surface.

Whether or not they have a protective coating, most cymbals eventually get dirty or tarnished. If you want them to look and sound as good as possible, you should clean them periodically. There used to be a false notion that cleaning a cymbal was detrimental to its sound. In earlier years, when there was not as much choice in cymbal sounds, many drummers allowed dirt and tarnish to build up on the surface of their cymbals. This inhibited the cymbal's resonance slightly and contributed to a warmer, mellower sound that was suitable for low volume levels. Drummers were then afraid to clean the cymbal for fear of losing this tonal quality. The main reason the cymbal sounded more mellow as it became dirtier, however, was due to natural changes in the crystal structure of the metal, due to age and constant striking. After the cymbal aged this way, it could have been cleaned and it still would have retained its warmer tone. (The traditional way of muffling a new cymbal that is too loud or has too much overtone is to apply a piece of tape to its underside. The length, width and placement of the tape determines the degree of muffling.) With the wide variety of cymbal sounds now available, careful selection can give you the sound you are looking for while keeping the cymbal clean so that it resonates freely.

Aside from the practical improvement in sound, keeping a cymbal shiny protects your investment. A clean, shiny cymbal has a better resale value than an identical, dirty, tarnished one. Also important at a time when the visual side of musical performance is so heavily emphasized is the difference in appearance that shiny cymbals make to your drumset.

It is impossible to predict how often your cymbals will require cleaning. Bronze tarnishes naturally but this is accelerated by the perspiration on your hands and by smoke, dust and pollution in the air. The more you handle and use your cymbals, the faster they will get tarnished and dirty. Some drummers may only need to clean their cymbals once a year, while others make it a monthly or even weekly affair. In general, more frequent light cleanings produce better results with less effort than major overhauls at long intervals.

The safest cleaner to use is one designed to remove dirt and tarnish without scratching or otherwise damaging the cymbal. Too much abrasion can change the surface molecular structure of the metal, adversely affecting the sound of the cymbal. Polishes are available from most cymbal manufacturers and from several accessory companies in the form of liquid, wadding, powder or paste. They can be divided into two basic categories: those that clean and polish by chemical action and those that use abrasion in addition to the chemical action. Avoid the abrasive cleaners unless you are faced with a cymbal that is so dirty and tarnished that repeated chemical cleaning alone does not give you good results.

Although it is possible to use any quality metal polish that is safe for bronze on many cymbals, some cymbal manufacturers specify their own formula. In some cases, they may specify different polishes for their different lines of cymbals. This is usually to avoid premature damage to a factory applied finish that is designed to keep the cymbal from tarnishing in the first place. For instance, Paiste's cymbal cleaner is designed to remove dirt from the surface of the cymbal without removing their protective wax-like coating. Any cymbal polish containing abrasives or acids would remove this coating. Once the coating has worn off, it may be necessary to use a cleaner that is better at removing tarnish.

Colored cymbals with delicate surface coatings should never be cleaned with any form of polish, as it may scratch or dissolve the color layer. They should be wiped occasionally with a soft, dry cloth. Colored cymbals should not tarnish, but if they are particularly dirty you can use warm water and mild soap to clean them.

Before special cymbal polish was readily available, drummers used other cleaners. Zildjian used to recommend the use of powdered household cleanser such as Ajax, Comet, etc. The powder could be rubbed dry into the grooves for light cleaning or with water in the consistency of paste for heavier cleaning. Use care if you try this method. Powdered cleansers are quite abrasive and can scratch the surface of a cymbal if used carelessly. To minimize this, be sure to rub along the grooves of the cymbal and never across them. Some drummers used to clean their cymbals with toothpaste, which is a mild abrasive. There are a number of other "home-remedy" methods. You should, however, use the polish recommended by the cymbal manufacturer or one of the other polishes designed specifically for cymbals to avoid the possibility of damaging your cymbals.

Rainbow Musical Products sells Buckaroo cymbal cleaner, a chemically impregnated cotton wadding that removes tarnish without abrasion. Slobeat sells a powdered cymbal cleaner. There are several others available. Check your music store or the advertisements in drum magazines.

Whatever polish you choose, follow the directions on the container. Apply it with a clean, soft cloth. Always work in the direction of the grooves left by the lathing process to avoid scratches. Remember to clean both the top and bottom of the cymbal. In many cases, the bottom is the side most easily seen by your audience when performing. Heavily tarnished cymbals may require several applications of polish before the results satisfy you. The edge of the cymbal (where you touch it while playing) is usually the dirtiest area. An old toothbrush or similar soft bristle brush can be used to rub the polish into the grooves in these heavily tarnished areas. Rub gently and follow the grooves to avoid scratches. Buff with a soft cloth to remove the polish.

Proper cleaning requires the use of a bathtub, laundry tub or sink with enough room to rinse your largest cymbal. Almost any cleaner leaves a residue on the cymbals that becomes noticeable under stage lights. You can avoid this problem by rinsing each cymbal after cleaning it. Use warm water and a sponge or soft, clean cloth to wash the polish residue out of the grooves. If the polish is not water-soluble, you may have to wash it off with liquid dishwashing soap before rinsing. Dry the cymbal immediately with a towel or soft, clean cloth to avoid renewed tarnish and water spots.

As a last step to prolong the effects of your work, you may want to apply a very light coat of spray furniture wax to the surface of the cymbal, as mentioned earlier. This seals the metal from contact with the air and your sweaty hands. Too much of this waxy coating will muffle a cymbal.

Some drummers consider buffing their cymbals with industrial polishing compound on a buffing wheel to remove tarnish and renew their appearance. This should only be done by an expert, if at all. Buffing removes a substantial amount of metal from the surface of the cymbal and creates a great deal of heat from the friction. Getting a cymbal too hot can ruin its sound and make it susceptible to cracking after it has cooled down. It is much better to use a cymbal polish to keep your cymbals looking good.

Some of the cymbal manufacturers publish catalogs, brochures or booklets explaining the differences between the many choices of cymbals they offer. In a few cases, they include advice about caring for their brand of cymbals. Obtain all the information you can find that will help you to make the best choice for your personal requirements.

You should always buy quality cymbals. The sound of a mediocre drum can be improved by fitting it with good quality heads, tuning it carefully, improving the bearing edge of the shell, etc. Where cymbals are concerned, what you hear initially is to a great extent what you are stuck with. Cymbals do mellow with age, but the sound of a poor quality cymbal will never satisfy you. You will eventually have to buy a better one to get a better sound. A good quality cymbal may be expensive but it will last for many years if properly used and maintained. Rather than buying a large set of poor quality cymbals, put your money into a basic set of good quality cymbals. You can later add to this one cymbal at a time. Good quality cymbals will inspire you to play better and will add immeasurably to the sound of your drumset.

Drumset Hardware

The term hardware, as applied to the drumset, refers to the legs, brackets, pedals, stands and holders that place the drums, cymbals and other accessories in position to be played. In the case of pedals, they are the devices used to play the drums or cymbals in question. These devices can be subdivided by function.

Bass Drum Spurs

Bass drum "spurs" (or legs) are attached to the shell of the drum at opposite sides, supporting it in playing position. There may be one or two pairs of spurs. One pair is usually sufficient but two pairs give more stability to bass drums with extra deep shells or bass drums that must support several toms, cymbals or other accessories. Originally, bass drum spurs were separate devices that clamped to the counterhoop of the bass drum and were not attached to the shell. There are two basic types in use on modern bass drums: folding spurs and retractable spurs. Folding spurs are attached to brackets on the bass drumshell and fold into a position parallel to the shell when not in use. Retractable spurs protrude from a bracket attached to the bass drumshell and retract through the bracket into the shell when not in use. Spurs are usually made from chrome plated steel.

In addition to their function of preventing any side-to-side motion of the bass drum, well designed spurs should also inhibit the tendency of the bass drum to creep forward when it is struck by the pedal beater. Spurs are usually equipped with sharp, metal spike ends to anchor firmly on carpeted surfaces. Most also feature a removable rubber cap or foot on the end of the spur for use on hard floor surfaces. Sometimes the rubber cap is threaded onto the spike so it can be retracted when the spike is needed. Rubber feet on all hardware are important because, in addition to providing

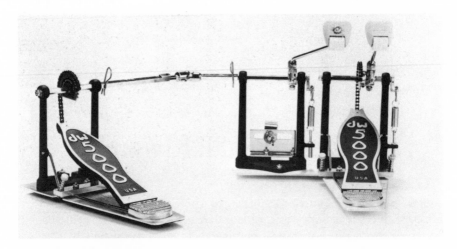

Drum Workshop double bass drum foot pedal. Notice offset beater on remote *(left)* **pedal, anti-creep adjustable spurs and stiffener plates under both pedals.** *(Courtesy of Drum Workshop.)*

a secure, non-slip grip for the equipment, they isolate it somewhat from vibrations carried through the floor.

Some spurs point straight from the shell to the floor when in position, while others are angled forward to assist in resisting bass drum creep. A friction device holds the spurs in the desired position. There are both light weight and heavy duty spur designs.

Clean and lubricate all threaded parts of the spur assembly periodically and replace rubber feet when they are worn or lost. Most failures in this piece of hardware occur because vibration loosens the fittings and drummers over-tighten them to prevent this from happening. The results are stripped threads and or cracked brackets. Some spur designs feature a memory clamp (a collar that tightens around the spur) which sets height or angle, taking most of the strain and making it unnecessary to over-tighten fittings. This also makes set-up quicker, but with retractable spurs it becomes necessary to remove and re-install the spurs at each set-up, rather than retracting them. If the spurs are not fitted with memory clamps, a hose clamp or plumber's clamp (available cheaply at most hardware stores) will serve the same function.

Floor Tom Legs

Floor tom legs are usually fitted in sets of three per drum. Sometimes very large floor toms (18″ or 20″ diameter) will have four legs attached.

Left: A Rims mount installed on a tom. The drum is suspended by its batter side hoop. *Right:* Rims mounts installed on floor toms, suspending them at the resonator side of the drum. *(Courtesy of Purecussion.)*

Many pieces of drum hardware have tripod (three-legged) bases because a tripod can adapt to an uneven floor surface without wobbling as a four-legged base would. The legs are held in place by brackets bolted to the shell of the drum. Most designs have a vertical hole in the bracket through which the leg passes. The leg is retained at the desired height by a friction device that tightens the leg against the bracket.

Floor tom legs are either solid steel rods (round or hexagonal) or hollow steel tubes. They are usually chrome plated and sometimes knurled for part of their length. Knurling (a small cross-hatch pattern engraved in the metal) creates a rougher surface for the bracket to hold, minimizing slippage. Legs are sometimes straight and sometimes angled at the bottom. Straight legs should be avoided when possible because they create a tripod only slightly larger than the diameter of the drum. The floor tom will not be very stable with this arrangement and can easily be knocked on its side. A better design is the leg that angles out away from the drum and then down again at its lower end. This creates a tripod significantly larger than the diameter of the drum for greater stability.

Most floor tom legs used to be a standard 16" long. The most common floor tom size is 16" × 16" and legs of the same length as the shell depth can be folded parallel to the shell for packing with no leg protruding at either end. This makes it easy to pack the drum in a case without removing the legs from their brackets. Unfortunately, it also limits the height adjustment of the drum. Some manufacturers now supply their floor toms with

longer legs that allow a greater range of height adjustment. The longer legs
will not fit in a case with the drum but they can be packed with the other
hardware. As with bass drum spurs, some floor tom legs are equipped with
memory clamps to quicken set-up and to prevent slippage and consequent
over-tightening. Hose clamps or similar devices can be used in this application if your floor tom legs are not supplied with memory clamps.

Clean and lubricate any threaded parts of the floor tom leg brackets
periodically and replace the rubber feet on the legs when they are lost or
worn. When the legs rest on a hard, solid floor, the resonance of the floor
tom may be adversely affected because the rubber feet are not providing
enough acoustic isolation. Resting each leg on a pad made of foam rubber
or other soft material to further isolate it from the floor is a trick that often
improves the sound. The rubber pads used by cellists and string bass
players for the same purpose are an excellent, commercially available solution to this problem.

Tom Holders or Mounts

The purpose of tom mounting hardware is to hold the drum securely
in a comfortable playing position. The hardware must be constructed
solidly enough to support the weight of the drum and withstand the force
of your playing style. It must also withstand the amount of setting up and
dismantling that you subject it to. It must incorporate enough range of
height and angle adjustment to position each drum where you want it. For
convenience and speed of set-up and dismantling, it should be possible to
set the mounting hardware at your desired position once, then simply
assemble the pieces each time to duplicate the initial setting exactly.

Toms are usually mounted in one of three ways: on the bass drum;
on a separate floor stand; or on a bracket attached to a cymbal stand. Single
toms in sizes up to 15" diameter can also be mounted on a snare drum
stand.

Older styles of bass drum mounts featured a curved tube (sometimes
called a rail) attached parallel to the curve of the bass drumshell. A metal
bracket encircled the tube and could slide along it, to be tightened in position wherever was most convenient. The upper portion of this bracket incorporated an angle adjustment and a short arm that fastened to a bracket
on the shell of the tom. This type of tom holder worked well enough within
its limitations. A combination of adjustments at several points was required to set the desired height and angle. There were two main disadvantages to this design which serve to illustrate the reasoning behind subsequent designs. First, height adjustment was very limited. Second, the

assembly could not be removed from the bass drum when dismantling, so it had to be folded against the shell to allow the drum to fit in a case. This made it necessary to re-set the assembly each time the drums were set up, taking extra time and creating extra wear on the component pieces of the tom holder.

Later developments used a bracket on the bass drum and a similar bracket on the tom connected by an L-shaped metal arm with a toothed gear or ball and socket joint somewhere on it. The vertical and horizontal portions of the arm protruded into the bass drum and tom shells, respectively. Height was adjusted by extending the vertical arm, angle was adjusted by the gear or ball and socket joint and lateral position was adjusted by extending the horizontal arm. The L-shaped arm could be removed and replaced without altering the angle setting and the later addition of memory clamps retained the settings for height and lateral position. This was obviously a big improvement, allowing greater range of adjustment and faster set-up.

Variations of this basic design dominate current models of tom mounts. Mounts designed to hold two toms commonly use a central vertical tube with two separate arms attached to the top of it. Although most designs use a vertical tube that telescopes into the bass drumshell, some manufacturers use a bracket on the exterior of the tom shell with a clamp for the tom arm, so it does not have to protrude into the tom shell. Some drummers feel that an arm projecting into the air column inside the tom shell will adversely affect the drum's sound. The only other possible disadvantage of having mounting hardware protrude into the shell of any drum is physical interference with an internally mounted microphone.

Some drummers find bass drum mounted tom holders inconvenient because their range of adjustment leaves the toms too close or too far away. The Corder Drum Company manufactures a Slide Trak tom mount with the vertical tube running in a track on the bass drum to move the toms closer or farther away from the drummer. By not projecting into the bass drumshell or tom shells, it also avoids interfering with the air column, an advantage for those drummers concerned with that feature.

Sometimes toms are mounted on a separate floor stand for reasons of convenient placement or to avoid mounting them on the bass drum. The concern is that the weight of large toms may create too much stress on the bass drumshell or inhibit its resonance. The base of this stand is usually identical to a heavy duty cymbal stand with the tom mount attached to the top. Care should be taken to position a tom stand so that one of the legs of the stand points in the direction that carries most of the weight of the toms. This makes the stand more stable. Larger toms that would usually be called floor toms are sometimes mounted on these stands singly or in

The Corder Slide Trak tom mount allows toms to be positioned closer or farther away from the drummer by sliding the mount in its track, which is mounted to the bass drumshell. *(Courtesy of Corder Drum Company.)*

pairs. Stand mounting sometimes may allow greater flexibility of height and angle positioning than the usual floor tom legs.

Most current tom holder designs allow the mounting of one or two toms. In some cases, there is a third mounting point on the holder to allow a third tom or cymbal holder to be mounted on the same assembly. With larger toms, heavy cymbals or extreme height or angle positioning, be sure that the assembly, including the bass drumshell is strong enough to handle the weight. Several manufacturers have offered internal extension tubes for their shell mounted tom holders. These tubes extend to the bottom of the bass drumshell, removing some stress from the area at the top of the shell that would otherwise have to support all this equipment. This is a useful option to consider, especially if you own very thin shell drums or if you ever perform with the resonator head and counterhoop removed from the bass drum. Without the counterhoop and head, there is less resistance to the shell deformation that can be caused by this excessive weight and stress.

Manufactured by Purecussion Inc., RIMS mounts are a type of mounting hardware that attach to your regular tom mounts. The letters R.I.M.S. stand for resonance isolation mounting system. A RIMS mount suspends a tom by means of a steel band that partly surrounds the drum. Several of the drum's tension rods pass through rubber grommets held by this band, thus supporting the drum from the batter side counterhoop without the need for any mounting hardware bolted to its shell. This is supposed to allow the drumshell to vibrate more freely, increasing the resonance of the drum and emphasizing its fundamental pitch. Any difference in sound is probably most noticeable from drums with thin shells or drums that are mounted on extremely rigid holders. By isolating each drum from the others, a RIMS mount does minimize the transference of sympathetic vibrations between drums through solid mounting hardware. Your ears are the best judge of whether or not there is any improvement in sound.

Two disadvantages (other than the significant cost of the product) are the added bulk of the RIMS mount, which might make it difficult to fit the drum into a case and the extra complication of changing a drumhead on a drum equipped with a RIMS mount.

Cymbal Stands

Cymbal stands must hold cymbals securely at a comfortable height and angle for easy reach. They come in four basic types:

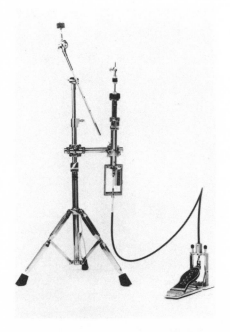

floor mount cymbal stand
floor mount boom cymbal stand
cymbal "hanger" stand
cymbal holder

Drum Workshop cable operated hi-hat stand designed for remote positioning of hi-hat cymbals. The upper section of the hi-hat stand is shown clamped to a boom cymbal stand. *(Courtesy of Drum Workshop.)*

Regular, boom and hanger cymbal stands have folding tripod bases with rubber feet on each leg of the tripod. The cymbal holder mounts on a bass drum, a tom mount or another cymbal stand.

Many types of drumset hardware are described as single or double braced. Single braced stands have the tripod base constructed from single, flat or tubular pieces of steel. Double braced stands use two pieces of flat steel to construct each leg of the tripod. Running two pieces of metal side by side and joining them at points along their length creates a stronger stand. Unfortunately, it also creates a heavier and bulkier stand that costs more. Your choice between single and double braced stands should be based on your requirements for strength and durability as well as on what you can afford.

Up to the mid–1970s, most cymbal stands were much lighter weight construction than the professional model stands now in use. A typical example is the flush-base stand. Its tripod folded open until the legs were almost parallel to the floor. Although this style of stand was very compact

Drum Workshop hi-hat stand with third leg of tripod base removed. This design allows greater freedom of placement for remote bass drum foot pedals close to the hi-hat stand. *(Courtesy of Drum Workshop.)*

and easily portable, it would not have enough height, strength or stability to withstand the heavier use that is expected from modern hardware.

The upright position of a cymbal stand is constructed from lengths of steel tubing with height adjustment achieved by using graduated diameters of tubing that telescope into one another. Tension devices are used at the top of each section to set the height. Better stands avoid metal to metal contact in this area by using plastic insert collars that grip the smaller diameter tubing when tension is applied. This avoids over-tightening and subsequent thread stripping, which was a common cause of breakage on older stands.

In addition, memory clamps may be fitted to retain height adjustment from set-up to set-up and to carry most of the weight of the upper sections. This simplifies and quickens set-up but requires you to disassemble the stand into sections for packing instead of telescoping it. It is a trade-off of one convenience for another. If your stands are not fitted with memory clamps and you would like to use them, hose clamps are an inexpensive substitute.

In general, older stands had less maximum height adjustment than do modern stands. Also, the tilting devices at the top that are an integral part of modern cymbal stands were once an option. The tilter is an important part of a cymbal stand. There are two basic designs of tilters: gear tooth types and friction types. Toothed angle adjustment uses two interfacing gears that are tightened together at the desired position. This is a very strong, non-slip method of setting the angle of a cymbal but it limits the setting to the angles at which the gear teeth align. Friction tilters have no gear teeth and can be set at any angle within their range of adjustment. They may be ball and socket or swivel mechanisms. Some designs might vibrate loose and slip during heavy use, however. Over-tightening to prevent this can break the mechanism. This is another design trade-off. If you can not get the exact angle you want with a gear tilter, a friction tilter is the answer, but be sure to select one that is well made to avoid slippage if you are a heavy player.

The very top of the stand where the cymbal is mounted must be properly equipped to prevent damage to the cymbal. A large metal washer is the main support for the cymbal. This washer should be convex in shape to fit under the bell of the cymbal. On top of this hard washer there should be a felt washer to isolate the cymbal from the stand. Felt washers are available at any well stocked music store and should be replaced when dirty, worn or badly compressed. The metal washer must not be larger than the felt washer or it may come into contact with the underside of the cymbal during heavy playing.

The shaft of the tilter that passes through the cymbal's mounting hole must be covered by a plastic or rubber sleeve to prevent the cymbal from contacting it. Check this sleeve regularly and replace it when it is worn. If you cannot find replacements at a music store, you can make them from clear plastic tubing of the type sold at auto parts stores. Check the diameter of the tilter shaft and purchase tubing with an inside diameter that will fit snugly over the shaft. Be sure the outside diameter of the tubing is not so large that it inhibits the movement of the cymbal. Only a couple of inches of tubing are needed for each stand, so a few feet of tubing in your spare parts kit will last you for a long time.

Many cymbal stands are equipped with a second felt washer designed to fit on top of the cymbal, under the wing nut. If you must mount a cymbal at an extreme angle where it may come into contact with the wing nut when it is struck, this second piece of felt is useful. If the cymbal is mounted close to horizontal, it is not needed and just muffles the cymbal unnecessarily. Sometimes over-tightened wing nuts press this piece of felt against the top of the cymbal. This inhibits free movement of the cymbal, leading to stress cracking. Always allow the cymbal to move freely by mounting it loosely.

As mentioned, wing nuts are the usual method of securing the cymbal to the stand. If you have ever wasted time searching for a dropped wing nut while setting up or dismantling your drumset, you will appreciate a small innovation that many manufacturers have put at the very top of the tilter shaft. Instead of starting the threads for the wing nut at the top of the shaft, the shaft is reduced in diameter at the top. This allows you to place the wing nut in position before trying to thread it onto the stand. This is a very small feature that is well worth looking for.

Three alternate methods of securing the cymbal to the stand are worth mentioning. Zildjian offers their Zil-Bel Cymbal Snap to replace the wing nut. It is a hinged wing nut that does not require removal from the stand when you remove or replace a cymbal. It folds vertically when you install or remove the cymbal and folds horizontally to keep the cymbal in place when you are performing. Unfortunately, it is only available for a certain shaft diameter and thread size that is not used on many modern stands. Tama offers their Cymbal-Mate to replace the metal wing nut. It is a plastic wing nut that self-taps onto most thread sizes. It incorporates a tubular extension that serves the purpose of the plastic shaft sleeve mentioned earlier. Identical devices (without the Tama name on them) are sold by accessory companies at approximately half the cost. Sonor makes a quick release cymbal lock that is installed or removed by squeezing it with your fingers. Its two halves clamp onto the tilter, held by an elastic strap. The plastic construction of the Tama and Sonor devices makes them less likely to cause damage than a metal wing nut if a cymbal does contact them.

Boom cymbal stands are simply normal floor mount stands with a lateral extension arm fitted at the top. This extension or "boom" allows the cymbal to be placed closer to the drummer than might be possible with the use of a regular stand. Especially with larger drumsets, it is often difficult to get a cymbal close enough for easy reach. There may be no room for the base of the stand or there may be drums positioned under the spot where you would like the cymbal. The lateral boom arm can solve these problems. A few companies make cymbal stands that convert from upright types to booms as needed. When the boom is not required, it retracts into the upright tube to be used as a vertical extension.

Cymbal hanger stands are an old idea re-cycled with newer technology. In photographs of early drumsets, you can see cymbals hanging on straps from lateral arms. Modern hanger stands are a type of boom stand that mounts (or suspends) the cymbal from the top instead of underneath. The intended advantage is that there is no hardware under the cymbal to interfere with other parts of the drumset. There are situations where this is more convenient, but many drummers buy them only because they look different. There is nothing wrong with that. Just be sure that the method of securing the cymbal to the hanger boom is quite secure or the vibration of playing could loosen it and drop the cymbal.

When you place the weight of a cymbal anywhere except directly over the center of its stand, striking the cymbal may tip the stand. Heavy duty boom stands usually have a counter-weight at the opposite end of the boom from the cymbal, effectively counter-balancing the cymbal and correcting this problem. Not all boom stands have counter-weights, though, and it is wise to position the legs of the tripod base so that one of the legs extends in the same direction as the boom. Tripod base stands usually allow the base to be spread as widely as is desired. The more lateral extension of

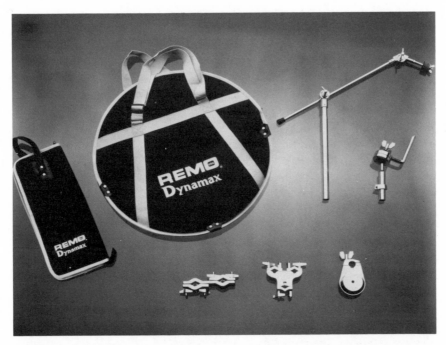

Examples of boom cymbal holder, tom mounting arm *(upper right)*, clamps for mounting accessories *(below)*. Also *(left to right)* stick bag and soft cymbal case. *(Courtesy of Remo, Inc.)*

the boom you use, the wider you should spread the legs. This will give the stand the greatest possible stability.

Boom stands feature two tilting devices: the usual one under the cymbal and another where the boom is attached to the stand. When a particularly long boom arm is used, it may be in two sections that telescope into each other for easier packing and transport.

Cymbal holders are basically cymbal stands without tripod bases. They are available in both straight and boom types and are mounted on the bass drumshell or on another piece of hardware. When four-piece drumsets were the standard of the industry, many bass drums came equipped with a cymbal holder mounted to the bass drumshell. This placed the ride cymbal in roughly the same position as the larger mounted tom on a five-piece drumset. Ludwig is one company that still has this type of cymbal holder available. It can also be mounted on the bass drum counterhoop with a clamp.

Current cymbal holder designs are usually the boom type. The vertical tube of the holder is attached by a clamp to any convenient piece of hardware and the boom provides lateral positioning. Using this device, two

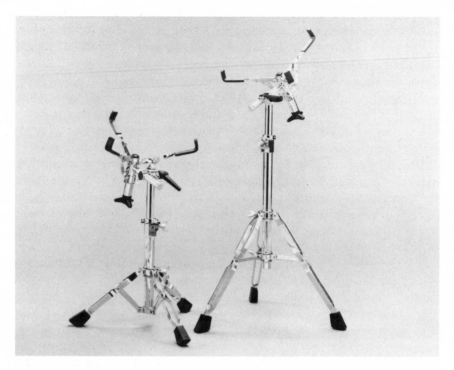

Drum Workshop snare drum stands showing offset basket for holding snare drum, double-braced legs, large rubber feet for stability and vibration insulation. *(Courtesy of Drum Workshop.)*

cymbals can be mounted on a single stand, reducing the amount and bulk of your hardware.

As with other hardware, clean and lubricate any threaded parts and replace worn or missing rubber feet on all your cymbal stands. At regular intervals, put a drop of oil on each swivel joint of the tripod base to keep them operating smoothly.

Snare Drum Stands

Snare drum stands have a tripod base, similar in design to that of a cymbal stand but usually much smaller. They are available in light or heavy duty designs, some single braced and others double braced. The legs of the stands are fitted with rubber feet. Many older snare drum stands, like older cymbal stands, had a light weight, flush base design.

Height adjustment is achieved by an upper tube that telescopes into the larger diameter base tube. The adjustment is set by a tension device, with plastic insert collars and memory clamps used on some models to avoid slippage. Angle adjustment near the top of the stand is provided by a gear tooth or friction tilting device. The same advantages and disadvantages of these two methods of operation apply to snare drum stands as they do to the tilters on cymbal stands.

The main variation in design of snare drum stands concerns the method of mounting the drum on the stand. This part of the stand, sometimes called the "basket," comes in two types. The simpler, lighter weight design has a central bracket with three arms. The arms at each side swivel out from the bracket, while the middle arm slides through the bracket. The snare drum is placed against the ends of the swivel arms and the middle arm is telescoped in to hold the drum in position. A friction screw is often used to keep the middle arm from sliding out of position as the drum is played. This design is light in weight and compact, folding quite small for packing. However, it allows the resonator head of the snare drum to rest very closely to the bracket, making it unsuitable for drums with more bulky snare mechanisms. Not many professional quality snare drum stands use this design any more.

The alternate design, which is widely used, was originally known as the "Buck Rogers" stand when it was introduced many years ago (it was named after the fictional futuristic hero, since it was considered a very advanced design). It has three identical folding arms attached to a central bracket. The arms fold together or apart in unison, controlled by a wing nut tensioner on a threaded stem at the bottom of the bracket. This design eliminates the problem of the stand interfering with the snares because only the ends of the arms come close to the snare drum. It also creates a more solid mounting for the drum. With the arms on the stand gripping the resonator side counterhoop of the drum, the snare drum can be lifted with the stand still firmly clamped to it.

The end of each arm on a snare drum stand is fitted with a rubber or plastic sleeve or foot that cushions metal to metal contact between the drum and the stand. These rubber or plastic pieces provide a more secure grip than a bare metal arm, helping to prevent the snare drum from slipping out of position. Substantial grip cushioning at this point also isolates the drum acoustically from the stand.

There are stands designed with extra height for playing a snare drum standing up. Other stands are designed with minimum height so that a 10″ deep snare drum can be mounted low enough for comfortable playing at the drumset. Every snare drum stand has a minimum and maximum usable height. Before you purchase a stand, be sure its range of height adjustment is adequate to position your snare drum at the height you want.

Ludwig drummer's thrones *(left to right)* lightweight throne, heavy-duty throne, heavy duty throne with back rest, seat case throne. *(Courtesy of Ludwig.)*

Thrones

"Drummer's throne" is the name commonly used for a stool designed for drumset use. Most thrones have a tripod base that folds up for packing. They must be kept clean and well lubricated like all other drumset hardware. There are lightweight and heavy-duty models, single or double braced. Each leg is fitted with a rubber foot and the vertical base tube has provision for height adjustment. On inexpensive, light weight models, a smaller diameter tube telescopes into the base tube, held at the desired height by a bolt running through it. This limits height adjustment to the pre-set intervals at which the bolt holes are drilled. More expensive models use a tension collar on the tube or a threaded rod like a piano stool to set height. These designs are more minutely adjustable.

A padded seat is attached to the top of the height extension tube or rod. More expensive thrones tend to have larger seats with thicker padding for more comfort. Most seats are vinyl covered but some manufacturers use woven fabric. Vinyl is easier to clean while woven fabric permits air circulation, making it cooler to sit on.

There are a few other notable variations in throne design. The first is the inclusion of a back rest with some models. The extra comfort of support for the lower back comes with the disadvantage of more weight and bulk to pack and transport. If you experience back pain after a long session at your drums, changing to a throne with a back rest may be well worth this extra trouble.

Another variation is the use of a differently shaped seat cushion. Although most throne cushions are round, a few manufacturers offer a more triangular shaped seat on some of their thrones. This bicycle saddle shape does not interfere as much with the motion of the drummer's thighs while playing, especially for drummers who sit quite high.

The last major variation is the seat case throne. This throne looks like a deep drumshell with a seat cushion at the top, which is exactly what it is. Seat case thrones are finished to match the rest of your drumset and look quite smart. They are also practical, as the seat cushion detaches to allow other drumset hardware to be stored and transported inside the seat case. The main disadvantage of this design is its non-adjustable height, usually about 24", which does not suit every drummer.

There are a few other things to consider when selecting a throne. Good thrones are expensive but worth the cost. The flimsy construction of some light weight models will not withstand professional use and is not as comfortable. Well made thrones are fairly solid, while poorly made thrones wobble and rattle. Maximum and minimum height adjustments vary from one model to another. Be sure that the one you select has the range of height adjustment you need. If you sit rather high or move around a lot as you play, you will need a wide tripod base to provide enough stability and to avoid tipping over.

Height adjustments that rely on a tension collar gripping a smooth tube or rod are more prone to slippage than other designs. If you weigh a lot or if you tend to bounce around as you play, avoid that kind of height adjuster. If the padding in the seat compresses completely, allowing you to contact the hard seat platform, you will not be comfortable. Look for a throne with firm padding that maintains some loft when you sit on it. If you already own a throne with this problem, it can be re-upholstered with better padding, perhaps at less cost than buying a new throne. You can even re-cover the seat yourself if you are handy at that type of work.

A comfortable, solid, sturdy throne that adjusts to the correct height for you will make playing easier and reduce fatigue. Because a throne is not included in the cost of most new drumsets, some drummers make do with a regular bar stool or a chair with a thick telephone book on the seat to increase the height. Or they buy the cheapest throne they can find, considering it to be an unimportant piece of equipment. Spend some time selecting a good throne and expect to pay as much as you would for any other piece of top quality hardware. Once you have experienced the difference it makes, you will know that the investment was worthwhile.

Rack Mounting Systems

A rack mounting system is a set of horizontal and vertical tubes to which other pieces of drumset hardware are attached. Racks are designed to mount large numbers of drums, cymbals, electronic pads and external microphones without the forest of stands that would otherwise be required. The predecessors of modern rack systems can be seen in photographs of drumsets from the 1920s and 1930s. A semicircular piece of tubing was attached parallel to the upper portion of the bass drumshell, with toms, cymbals, wood blocks, cow bells and temple blocks mounted on it. In the 1960s, the innovative but little known Flat Jacks drums used a similar straight tube on top of the bass drum to mount toms, cymbals and accessories. Like many other developments in drumset hardware, racks are a new variation of an old idea.

Modern rack systems are usually self-supporting, with vertical support tubes attached to horizontal cross tubes. Others clamp the horizontal tubes to existing cymbal stands on the drumset. Elaborate versions completely surround the drummer with tubing. Mounting clamps are tensioned on the tubes in the desired locations to hold drumset components. Tube diameters and clamp designs vary from one manufacturer to another. If you are contemplating the purchase of one of these systems, check that the rack hardware is compatible with the drumset hardware you intend to mount.

Although a rack system can be used on the simplest drumset, its cost is best justified when used on larger, more elaborate drumsets. One of the functions of a rack system is to eliminate much of the conventional hardware that would otherwise be required. The larger the drumset, the more hardware can be eliminated. Some racks are quite expensive. If the rack system actually costs more than conventional hardware, it should provide other benefits to compensate for the increased cost.

A well designed rack system should guarantee consistent placement of drumset components from one set-up to the next. Some form of memory clamps attached to the bar sections make this easier to achieve. Vertical tubes with height markings also speed set-up and make exact duplication of settings possible with minimum fuss. End support clamps for the horizontal bars that remain attached to the bars during transport maintain the rotational angle of the bar from one set-up to the next. Without this feature, setting up a rack will be more time-consuming and potentially less accurate than the use of conventional hardware.

To maximize stability, the horizontal tubes of a rack system should be mounted level and as low as is practical. Improper leveling or extreme bar height raises the center of gravity and decreases stability. Long sections of tubing are awkward to pack and transport in a small vehicle. Some manufacturers use bar connectors between shorter lengths of tubing. The provision of adjustable angle selection at these connections can make the shorter tubing more versatile and adaptable to individual drumset configurations.

Some rack systems use V-shaped prism clamps to attach equipment to the tubes. When tightened firmly, they can exert too much pressure in one area and dent the tubing. If possible, avoid them in favor of exact-sized circular design clamps that exert pressure evenly around the tube.

Using a rack system involves removing all toms, cymbals and other items from their usual mounts on the bass drum. This can be an advantage or disadvantage. With nothing attached to the bass drum, it is acoustically isolated from other drumset components. With no additional weight to hold it down, however, it may tend to creep forward as you play it. If you experience this problem, it may be possible to secure the bass drum to the rack in order to maintain its position. Hi-hat stands can also be clamped to rack systems to prevent them from sliding during use.

Racks have a high-tech look that has become very popular. Many drummers buy them simply because they like the way they look. There is nothing wrong with this as long as you do not sacrifice convenience and function in the process. If you are sure that a rack is the logical choice for you, become familiar with the various designs and decide which provides the best combination of cosmetic appeal and function for your needs. Component design differs from one manufacturer to another. Quality and price also vary, so comparison shopping can be very enlightening.

Hi-Hat Stands

Hi-hat stands are more complex than other stands that just hold a drum or cymbal in position. A hi-hat stand is actually operated by the drummer during performance. Smooth trouble-free operation is the primary requirement from a hi-hat stand.

The name "hi-hat" is explained by the history of this stand's development. The original device used in the 1920s was called a "sock symbal." Descriptions vary, but basically it consisted of two small cymbals mounted facing each other on short boards. The boards were hinged together at one end and sat on the floor with the drummer's foot on the top board. By means of a spring between the boards or a strap for the drummer's foot on the top board, the cymbals were held apart or struck together. Refinements of this idea resulted in a device called a "low-boy," which was similar to a modern hi-hat stand but only one or two feet high. Increasing the height of a low-boy allowed the drummer to play on the cymbals with sticks in addition to operating them with the foot. This taller pedal became known as a "hi-sock" or "hi-hat."

A modern hi-hat has a foot pedal at the bottom of a vertical tube. A folding tripod base fitted with rubber feet provides stability. The bottom cymbal rests upside down on top of the vertical tube. The top cymbal is mounted on a pull rod that runs down the middle of the vertical tube. At the bottom of the tube, the pull rod is attached to the foot pedal. Pressing on the foot pedal pulls the top cymbal into contact with the bottom cymbal. A spring returns the top cymbal to its resting position when the foot pedal is released.

Although that brief description covers the basic function, there are several refinements to the design. The height of the stand is adjusted by constructing the vertical tube in two sections and telescoping the upper section into the base. Height adjustment is maintained by a friction device at the top of the lower tube, with most stands including a memory clamp to prevent slippage or over-tightening. On more expensive models, spring tension is adjustable to vary the degree of force necessary to press the pedal.

Most hi-hat stands have an adjustable spur or other anchoring device somewhere on the base. Pressure on the pedal drives the spur against the floor or carpet, preventing the stand from sliding away from the drummer during use. The footboard may be a single piece design or it may be hinged in the middle with a separate heel plate. Some footboards have a toe stop at the front for the drummer's shoe to rest against. The front of the footboard is attached to the pull rod by means of a fabric, plastic or metal strap or by a short piece of bicycle chain.

The bottom cymbal sits on a felt washer on top of a flat or concave rest that may be part of the vertical tube or a separate piece. All good hi-hat stands incorporate a tilting device in this area that lifts one side of the bottom cymbal to adjust its angle of contact with the top cymbal. This prevents air from being caught between them and muffling the sound. The tilting device is usually operated by a thumb screw.

The top cymbal is held loosely between two felt washers on the hi-hat clutch. The clutch may be positioned high or low on the pull rod to adjust the gap between the cymbals and the corresponding stroke length of the pedal. It is held in position by a friction screw.

Because a hi-hat has moving parts, it is particularly important to keep it clean and well lubricated. The most common causes of trouble on a hi-hat stand include the pull rod (which will not function smoothly if it is bent), the clutch (on which threaded parts strip due to over-tightening and lack of lubrication) and the point of attachment between the foot

Drum Workshop pedals and stands showing the options available with remote bass drum pedals and hi-hat stands. *(Courtesy of Drum Workshop.)*

pedal and the bottom of the pull rod (which is prone to breakage during heavy use).

Another potential problem is spring fatigue. Whenever you are not performing, release the clutch and allow the top cymbal to rest on the bottom cymbal. The spring will wear out much faster if it supports the weight of the top cymbal when it is not necessary. Keeping the cymbals together when the drumset is not in use also makes the hi- hat less tempting for people who like to play with unattended drumsets.

Supposedly, the original intention was for right handed drummers to operate the hi-hat stand with their left foot and play the hi-hat cymbals with their left hand. Ambidexterous playing has never caught on with the majority of drummers, who prefer to cross their right hand over their left and play the hi-hat cymbals with their right hand. In order to allow the left hand sufficient room to strike the snare drum in this situation, hi-hat stands must be capable of mounting the cymbals substantially higher than the height of the snare drum. Many earlier hi-hats had insufficient height adjustment for this. Most modern hi-hat stands have more than adequate maximum height but individual requirements vary, so you should check this before buying any particular stand.

There have been a number of different designs of hi-hat stands for special applications. Drum Workshop is one company that offers a hi-hat stand with a swiveling tripod base to keep the legs of the hi-hat from interfering with double bass drum pedals or other hardware. Hi-hat stands with joints in their vertical tubes have been tried, permitting the whole top of the stand to be tilted toward the drummer. Legless hi-hat stands are offered by many manufacturers for drummers who use two bass drums. The absence of a bulky tripod base permits the stand to be clamped to the second bass drum close beside the bass drum pedal for easier access.

Special clutches are available for double bass drummers, allowing you to drop the top cymbal with a stroke of your drumstick and lift it into position again by pressing and releasing the hi-hat pedal. This permits the double bass drummer to play on closed hi-hat cymbals while operating two bass drum pedals and switch to foot operation of the hi-hat without stopping to adjust the clutch by hand.

For drummers who prefer not to cross one hand over the other to play hi-hat cymbals, a remote hi-hat stand is the answer. The base of the stand is operated by the same foot as usual, but the top section of the stand holding the cymbals is clamped to a convenient location on the opposite side of the drumset. The pedal is connected to the cymbals by a flexible cable. Another way of accomplishing this is by using a normal hi-hat position and an auxiliary set of hi-hat cymbals mounted on the opposite side of the drumset. This second set of cymbals cannot be opened and closed, but is played in the permanently closed position when needed.

A hi-hat stand must be sturdy enough and high enough for your style of playing. There are lightweight and heavy-duty models available, both single and double braced. The stand's operation must be smooth and not too hard or soft for the speed you require and the weight of cymbals you use. It must have a tilter for the bottom cymbal and a sturdy, reliable clutch for the top cymbal. The choice between single-piece and two-piece pedal footboards is one of personal preference. There must be some form of anchoring device to keep the stand from sliding as you bounce your foot on it.

Bass Drum Pedals

The bass drum pedal is a particularly important part of the drumset. The way in which it responds to your foot has a substantial effect on your speed and technique. For that reason, many drummers insist on using their own bass drum pedal when playing a strange drumset. Reading and understanding the following explanation of pedal design should give you the necessary information to experiment intelligently until you achieve the feel you like with your pedal. A professional quality pedal, properly adjusted, should be totally reliable and effortless to play. The more experience you have as a drummer, the more thought you will put into the selection of the correct pedal.

The purpose of a bass drum pedal is to convert the movement of your foot into a stroke on the bass drum batter head. Notwithstanding the trend to call bass drums "kick" drums, we still require a mechanical device to accomplish this. Common pedal design (which has changed very little from some of the earliest pedals) turns the downward pressure of your foot against the pedal footboard into rotary motion that swings a pedal beater through an arc into contact with the batter head.

Pedals use some combination of base casting, footboard, horizontal shaft, spring and beater. Several of these are moving parts subject to wear and requiring regular maintenance to continue functioning properly. Many drummers ignore their pedal from the day they buy it until the day it fails. Then they complain, think they made a poor choice and repeat the process with their next pedal. The fact that many pedals last for years with such treatment is a tribute to their quality.

Assuming that parts remain available, it is possible to select a professional quality pedal, keep it clean and lubricated, replace worn or broken parts when necessary and use it for the rest of your drumming days. Most pedal failures are preceded by a long period of neglect and could be prevented with routine inspection and care. When a pedal breaks, it is usually in the middle of a performance. Understanding the design of your pedal and keeping it adjusted and maintained will improve its reliability and make it easier to play.

Bass drum pedals all use some form of clamp to connect them to the batter side counterhoop of the bass drum. In the simplest variation, the counterhoop is pinched between the base casting and a finger-tightened clamp. Different counterhoop thicknesses and ranges of counterhoop clamp adjustment from one manufacturer to another make it advisable to check for proper fit before buying. This is unlikely to be a problem if both the bass drum and the pedal are manufactured by the same company.

The wing nut that tightens the counterhoop clamp is usually located

The **Gig Rug** provides a carpeted surface to prevent scratching of the bass drum and sliding of stands. Bass drum creep is prevented by the built-in bumper. Position of stands can be marked on the rug to aid precise set-up. *(Courtesy of L.T. Lug Lock, Inc.)*

under the front of the pedal footboard. More convenient designs locate this adjuster on the side of the base casting so that it is not necessary to reach under the footboard. On a few models, clamp tension can be set initially and the pedal installed and removed by flipping a lever at the side of the pedal. The drawbacks associated with these more convenient designs are increased cost and the use of more moving parts that require occasional inspection and lubrication.

The area of the counterhoop where the bass drum pedal is clamped receives a great deal of wear. You can minimize this by purchasing a package of mole-skin in the foot care section of a pharmacy. This soft, self-adhesive material can be cut to suitable size and stuck to the counterhoop to protect it. When the mole-skin becomes worn or excessively dirty, remove it and stick on a fresh piece. The obsolete Rogers Swiv-O-Matic pedal used a clamp that was left in position on the bass drum counterhoop. The pedal fit into place on the clamp and was secured by a thumbscrew. This minimized bass drum counterhoop wear and located the pedal in exactly the same position every time it was installed. This idea is not being used on any pedals currently in production.

Many pedals feature a pair of adjustable spurs in the base casting that project against the floor or carpet, preventing the bass drum from sliding forward when it is struck. This is a simple, but very useful feature that is quite effective in correcting an annoying problem. On hard surfaces, only the very tips of these spurs should protrude. On carpet, they must protrude further to hook into the soft surface.

The base casting of a pedal has either one or two vertical posts to support a horizontal shaft. Most pedals mount the shaft between two posts. This provides firm support but permits no height adjustment for different diameter bass drums. Single post designs are often two pieces with the upper half of the post telescoping into the lower half to adjust pedal height. This is a useful feature if your bass drum is larger or smaller than the current standard of 22″ diameter. Other adjustments can sometimes be made to compensate for different drum sizes, such as using extra-long beater shafts on bigger drums, but this has an effect on the "feel" or action of the pedal.

The horizontal shaft at the top of a single or double post casting must be able to rotate smoothly to swing the beater through its arc. Most manufacturers mount the shaft on ball bearings or occasionally needle roller bearings. These bearings are subject to considerable stress and require occasional cleaning and re-lubrication. After careful removal, they should be soaked in a solvent to remove all dirt and old lubricant. When they have dried completely, examine them and replace them if they are badly worn or corroded. If not, apply a suitable grease lubricant and reinstall them. The shaft should now rotate smoothly and quietly. Except in cases of constant, severe use or particularly dirty playing environments, this operation should not be necessary more than once per year.

Attached to the horizontal shaft is a small casting known as the pedal cam that holds the pedal beater. On some pedals, like the Ludwig Speed King model, the shaft and cam are one piece. The beater is held in place by a tension screw operated by hand or by a drum tuning key. Beater shaft length is adjusted by sliding the beater shaft through the hole in the cam and tightening it in position to strike the bass drum at the desired spot, usually at or near the center of the head.

The cam is also the point of attachment between the rotating shaft and the pedal footboard. A metal or fabric strap or a length of bicycle chain connects the toe of the footboard to the cam. Leather was the traditional material in this application, but its tendency to stretch or break under heavy use led to the adoption of more durable materials. It should be possible to adjust the length of the strap to raise or lower the toe of the footboard for individual preference. Chain or hinged metal straps should be lubricated regularly to maintain smooth, quiet operation. The strap is one of the most failure-prone areas of the bass drum pedal and should be inspected regularly for wear.

The shape of the cam to which the strap is attached influences the way

Ludwig bass drum foot pedals *(left to right)* Speed King, Modular, Rocker, Rocker 2. Notice design differences. *(Courtesy of Ludwig.)*

the pedal feels in use. In some cases, the strap or chain runs over a round sprocket. This creates a linear relationship between footboard movement, spring tension and beater arc. Different shapes of cams change this relationship at different points along the arc of the beater stroke. Some experimentation with this in mind when you are selecting your next pedal will help you to understand why some pedals feel so different.

Pedal footboards are available in two designs: single piece or two piece hinged with separate heel plate. The choice is a matter of personal preference. Some footboards also have a toe stop for the drummer's shoe to rest against. An interesting design feature seen only on Ludwig's Speed King model is its convertible footboard that can be changed from single piece to hinged or vice versa by adjusting one screw on the bottom of the footboard. Whether one- or two-piece design, all footboards have a rear pivot point that is often neglected and should be lubricated regularly.

Underneath the footboard, a metal strap or rod connects the base casting to the heel of the footboard. This holds the footboard in position as it is played. On the Rogers Swiv-O-Matic pedal, this rod had a pivot point where it joined the base casting, allowing the drummer to locate the heel of the footboard left or right of dead center. This feature was useful to drummers who found it awkward to sit facing the bass drum with their foot exactly perpendicular to the batter head. This feature is not available on any current model pedals.

To add rigidity to the pedal for heavy playing, some models have the base casting and heel plate bolted to a metal support plate. While this undoubtedly creates a stronger assembly, it also prevents you from folding the pedal for convenient packing.

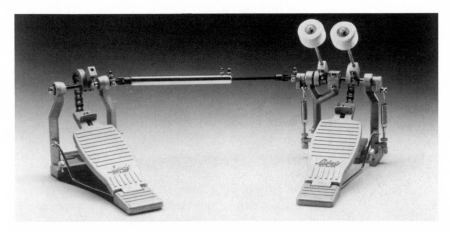

Ludwig Modular double bass drum foot pedal. Notice two universal joints on connecting shaft, single pedal base casting holding two beaters. *(Courtesy of Ludwig.)*

To return the beater to its original position after a stroke, one or two springs are used. Most pedal springs are attached to the exterior of the base casting and function by stretching. One exception is the Ludwig Speed King model, which uses compression springs inside hollow vertical posts on the base casting. Springs are another failure-prone part of pedal design. Any pedal spring is subject to metal fatigue after long or hard use. All will eventually lose some of their tension, but compression springs are less likely to break than stretched springs. A spare pedal spring is a handy item to carry in your spare parts kit. If you store a bass drum pedal for any length of time, loosening the spring tension will extend spring life.

The majority of pedals locate their springs in one of two places. The most common design uses a bracket at one or both ends of the horizontal shaft for the upper point of attachment. The spring is usually hooked to a threaded bolt at the lower end to facilitate tension adjustment. This spring assembly runs parallel to the vertical post and through a lug on the base casting. Tension is adjusted to your preference by loosening or tightening a nut at the lower end of the assembly. The upper point of attachment in this system features a selection of holes in the bracket. Your choice of hole affects the length of the beater's arc, influencing the feel or response of the pedal.

The other usual design is an upward extension of the bracket. There are two advantages to this system. Spring tension adjustment is more accessible, due to the uppermost location of the adjuster. Beater stroke length (the previously mentioned length of the beater's arc) is adjustable over a wider range and with greater precision by rotating the bracket backwards or forwards. Calato's Regal Tip model foot pedal uses this type of spring adjustment with the innovation of a double length spring that is adjustable at both ends to control both the stroke and the return of the beater.

One very popular design innovation is the double bass pedal. For drummers who want to play bass drums with both feet without buying or carrying a second bass drum, this is the answer. A double bass pedal has two beaters, the second beater controlled by a remote pedal. The main pedal is clamped to the bass drum in the normal manner. The remote pedal is placed next to the hi-hat pedal for easy access. A linkage connects both "halves" of the double pedal.

The pedal linkage telescopes for length adjustment and has one or more U-joints, usually at each end of the linkage, for angle adjustment. The remote pedal may be mounted on a support plate and or clamped to the hi-hat stand for stability. Some experimentation with beater stroke length and spring tension is necessary to achieve a similar response from both pedals. To avoid obtaining different sounds from each beater, both should be adjusted to strike in the same area of the batter head.

Miscellaneous Hardware

There are a few small items of drumset hardware that deserve to be mentioned but do not merit separate sections. The first of these is the bass drum anchor or, as it is often called, the bass drum creeper. If your bass drum slides away from you as you play and the combination of bass drum spurs and pedal spurs are not effective in correcting the problem, try one of these devices. It consists of a clamp that fits onto the bass drum resonator side counterhoop. Fitted on this clamp are two short metal rods with spikes at one end and rubber feet at the other. The spikes or rubber feet are adjusted to rest against carpet or hard floor, respectively. When the drum begins to slide, the spikes or rubber tips are driven against the floor, preventing further movement. These items are available from several manufacturers.

The next item is the stick holder, such as the Pro-Mark Stick Depot. This is a pair of tubes attached to a spring clamp. The spring clamp can be mounted on almost any piece of drumset hardware tubing. The tubes hold a pair of drumsticks, brushes or mallets in a convenient location for the drummer who must make quick stick changes or needs a spare pair ready to grab. An alternative to this is the counterhoop-mounted stick holder available from Ludwig (and possibly other manufacturers). This consists of a large spring attached in a horizontal position to a clamp that fits at the top of the bass drum batter side counterhoop. Several sticks can be wedged into the coils of the spring, holding them close to hand. These devices are designed to save the time of looking through your stick bag when you have just dropped a stick and must keep playing. They should not be regarded as a viable replacement for the stick bag.

The Sta-Way drum bumper made by Corder and the drum bumper made by Danmar are examples of a solution to the problem of closely mounted drums bumping or scraping each other. This is often a problem between the snare drum and the tom directly in front of it. Both devices attach to a drum by removing one tension rod and re-installing it through the hole in the bumper. A small, non-marring plastic or rubber cushion projects out from this point, preventing damage if the drums come in contact in this area. These items are inexpensive and can save delicate drum finishes.

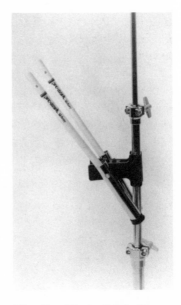

The Pro-Mark Stick Depot clips onto stands, holds a pair of sticks, brushes or mallets within easy reach. Useful for drummers whose work requires fast stick changes. *(Courtesy of Pro-Mark Corp.)*

Drumset Hardware Maintenance

Most drumset hardware is made from chrome plated steel. Chrome plating looks good and resists rust. In some cases, for cosmetic reasons, items of hardware are painted or anodized in different colors. When this equipment is new, it looks very distinctive, but anodized and (especially) painted finishes are not as durable as chrome plating. After being assembled, disassembled and transported many times, they show scratches and chips more readily than does good quality chrome plating. This not only ruins the appearance of the hardware but makes it more susceptible to rust where the finish has worn off.

Another disadvantage of colored hardware is its limited availability. Colored finishes on stands are offered for reasons of fashion on a limited number of items. This limits your choice of hardware to the pieces produced in that color by that one manufacturer if you want them to match. When the fashion changes, you may be unable to replace or add hardware

Sonor Protec alloy hardware with silver anodized finish, examples of *(left to right)* **floor stand for mounted toms, cymbal stand, hi-hat stand, snare drum stand.** *(Courtesy of Korg U.S.A.)*

in a matching finish. With chrome plated hardware, you can select the items you want from various manufacturers without being concerned about matching a finish.

An exception to the rule of chrome plated steel is Sonor's line of Protec hardware, made from a metal alloy that is supposed to be stronger than aluminum. It is lighter than comparable steel hardware, not susceptible to rust and comes with a silver-colored satin finish.

Keeping hardware clean and well lubricated lets it function smoothly and quietly and prolongs its life. Properly cleaned and maintained hardware also looks better and is worth more if you sell it or trade it for new equipment.

To do a thorough cleaning job, it is sometimes necessary to disassemble stands and pedals to their component parts. The only tools you are likely to need are your drum tuning key, an Allen wrench or a screwdriver. Some pedals that use Allen screw inserts come with the correct size Allen wrench, which is a useful idea.

Pay attention to the order and position of parts as you remove them and they will go back together easily. Draw diagrams for reference as you work if it will help you. Your dealer should have a spare parts catalog for your brand of hardware and sometimes you can obtain a copy of this from the manufacturer. It shows detailed diagrams of stands and pedals that make assembly and disassembly easy. In addition, a parts catalog provides you with part numbers and names for any bits and pieces that need replacement. With these numbers in hand, you can order replacement parts for your drums and hardware without guesswork.

Any good metal polish suitable for use on chrome plating will remove most of the dirt, tarnish or rust from your hardware. The fastest, most effective and least messy type is the chemically impregnated cotton wadding type, which is a chemical cleaner rather than an abrasive cleaner. Instead of scouring the surface, it dissolves the grime. Tear off a piece of the cotton wadding, rub it over the chrome and buff off the haze with a clean, soft cloth. It leaves little or no residue in hard to reach areas. One example of this is Buckaroo Cymbal Cleaner from Rainbow Musical Products which, as its name implies, is also suitable for cleaning cymbals.

To preserve the chrome, avoid using abrasives unless there is rust or dirt that resists chrome polish. In that case, rub the rusty or dirty area gently with very fine steel wool. If you are gentle, this will not damage the chrome and it is an effective abrasive. Finish with chrome polish and buff to a shine.

Many stands have rivets holding their parts together. These rivets may also be pivot points, allowing the stand to fold for packing. Constant use, especially with insufficient lubrication, loosens the rivets and the stand becomes wobbly. To prevent this problem from developing, put a drop of oil at each pivot point when the stand is new. Oil these points at regular intervals to smooth their operation and decrease wear. Because most light machine oils tend to run off, try one of two alternatives. Most brands of motorcycle chain oil are designed to flow on like oil and dry to a grease-like consistency. Several brands are available and they solve the runny oil problem for most applications on drumset hardware. Latin Percussion sells an oil with similar properties that they call Lug Lube, which comes in convenient, small applicator bottles and is available at many music stores.

If the rivets on your hardware are already loose, they can be tightened by careful peening of the flattened side of the rivet with a ball peen hammer. Spread the rivet just enough to take up the slack, but not so much that the joint becomes stiff. Heavy peening can crack rivets, however.

If your stands have any stripped fasteners, missing or worn out compression collars, rubber feet or sleeves on snare drum stand arms, replace these items with new parts. Inexpensive hose clamps can be used to set stand height, taking much of the weight and reducing the necessity to over-tighten fittings.

Occasionally, you may over-tighten a wing nut and find it difficult to loosen by hand. Try this old drummer's trick. Place one drumstick on each side of the wing nut and hold the sticks together with one hand at each end. Twisting the drumsticks gives you plenty of leverage to loosen the fitting.

If you have a substantial amount of hardware that must be disassembled into sections each time you pack it, you can waste a lot of time figuring out which pieces fit together. Buy a package of small, self-adhesive stickers in several colors at a stationery or office supplies store. Choose one color of sticker for each stand and attach a sticker of that color to each section of the stand. When you set up, match stickers of the same color to find the component pieces of each stand.

Make it a habit to inspect your hardware at regular intervals. Small problems tend to turn into serious problems if neglected. Good quality equipment maintained with care and attention on a regular basis will save you time, money and trouble.

Drumset Cases

A drumset is a substantial investment. Many drummers neglect to budget for the purchase of cases when they buy the rest of their equipment. Protecting equipment pays off in longer life, less maintenance expense, better resale value and greatly improved appearance.

The simplest form of protection for the drummer who keeps his or her drums set up or stored at home is a drop cloth spread over the entire drumset. Drums are great dust collectors and will require far less frequent cleaning if they are covered when not in use. This is also a good idea for the drummer who plays in night clubs where the drums remain set up for more than one night. At home or on stage, covering your drums has the added benefit of discouraging people who cannot resist tampering with an unattended drumset. Do not use a plastic drop cloth. Moisture in the air can condense under a plastic sheet and cause rust damage. Most other fabrics allow air to circulate and will not trap moisture. Bed sheets make handy drop cloths. The larger your drumset, the bigger the size of bed sheet. Wash the drop cloth periodically so it will not deposit accumulated dust on your drums if it is flipped over.

If you store your drums for any length of time, covering them with a drop cloth is the very least you should do. Packing them in some type of cases provides much better protection and keeps small items together during storage to prevent loss.

Transporting your drumset without cases can destroy it in a very short time. Using cases will help to keep your drumset in good shape for as long as you own it. There are four main reasons to pack your drumset in some type of cases when you must move it:

1. To minimize damage due to bumping, scratching, dropping and piling one piece of equipment on top of another. Regardless of how carefully you carry your drums to your vehicle, they are going to be bumped around as you drive to the performance.

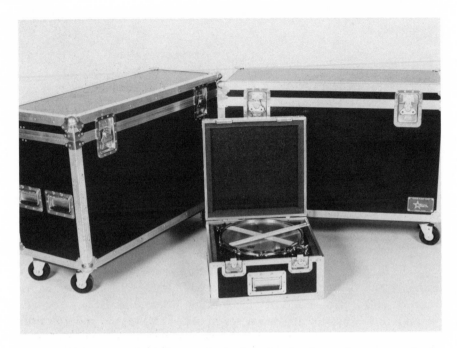

Large drum trunks and small snare drum case showing heavy-duty caster wheels, recessed handles and locking latches. *(Courtesy of Gold Star.)*

2. To protect your equipment from the weather and other atmospheric hazards. Rain, snow, freezing cold, intense heat and dusty or polluted air are not good for drums, cymbals or hardware. Even strong sunlight will eventually fade and yellow the finish on drums.

3. To make packing, carrying and transporting easier. You will need fewer trips to the car. The hardware can be packed in one box. Smaller cases can be stacked on top of a case with wheels and rolled in with no damage. Cases also simplify packing your vehicle because you do not have to worry about loose items bumping each other.

4. To organize your equipment and deter loss or theft. Using a checklist (that can be taped inside the lid of one of the cases) as you pack each case avoids the problem of forgotten items left on the stage. It also avoids the frustration of arriving at the performance and finding out that some essential piece of equipment is still at home.

Cases make your drumset less noticeable while it is in your vehicle. On stage, when you are setting up or packing, dishonest people can cause individual pieces of equipment to "disappear," but walking off with a whole drum case that is clearly marked with your name, address and phone number is more obvious. If you do forget something, a case

Ludwig hard fiber bass drum case *(left)* and molded plastic tom and bass drum cases *(middle and right).* Notice the folding steel side handles on the molded plastic drum case, a useful feature for larger cases. *(Courtesy of Ludwig.)*

with a luggage tag or other marking will help an honest person return your equipment to you.

Sizes

Ready made cases are designed to carry a specific size of drum or cymbal. A cymbal case that is marked 20″, for example, is designed to hold cymbals up to a maximum diameter of 20″. Even if all the cymbals are within the maximum diameter for which the case is built, large numbers of cymbals or those with bulky designs (such as Chinese cymbals with their upturned edges) could overload the case or require a larger case.

Similarly, drum cases are designed for a specific size of drumshell, with extra clearance left for the tuning hardware, heads, counterhoops, mounting hardware, etc. When you buy a 9″ × 13″ tom case, for example, it should fit a tom with those shell dimensions. Variations in the size and shape of hardware attached to the shell by different manufacturers will make some drums of the same shell size fit tightly and others fit loosely in the same case. Try fitting your equipment into a case before buying it.

Some hard drum cases are telescopic (designed to fit a specific diameter of drumshell with provision for expanding or contracting to fit differing shell depths). This type of case has an extra-deep lid that telescopes onto the main section of the case until it encounters the top of the drum. This is how some case manufacturers cope with the variety of shell sizes since the introduction of extended shell depths. It eliminates the problem of making a case for each possible increment of shell depth, which keeps costs reasonable. The only potential problem with this design is that with deeper shell drums, the drum is used to limit the telescoping of the case lid. Only the shallower shell drums have space between the drum and the ends of the case. This reduces protection for the deeper drums and makes interior padding of the ends of the case very important. If cost is not prohibitive, a case sized for exact depth as well as diameter eliminates this problem and provides better protection.

Types

There are several types of cases available. They differ in materials and construction, weight, bulk, durability, cost and level of protection. Any drummer who must transport his or her drumset from place to place should invest in some type of cases.

The best protection is the A.T.A. (Airline Transport Association) rated flight case. These are the heavy-duty cases used by most big name touring bands for all their equipment. They are available ready made from some companies, although most are custom built. Individual cases can be made for each drum or the whole drumset can be contained in one large trunk-like case.

Flight cases are constructed from plywood with a protective outer layer of plastic, fiberglass or aluminum. Extruded aluminum edges, steel corners, large caster wheels and heavy-duty hinges, handles and locking hardware are used. This style of case is designed to protect your drums during rough handling by road crews and commercial carriers. They are heavier, bulkier and more expensive than other cases but offer more protection. They can be provided with locks to prevent theft of the contents during transport or storage.

Not all flight cases are the same quality, although they may look the same to the casual observer. If you are serious enough to invest the time and money to obtain the best protection, be sure you are getting it. The plywood should be at least one-quarter inch thick. Thicker plywood is sometimes used and will increase protection, weight and cost, but anything thinner will not withstand long use.

Plastic is currently the most commonly used material for the outer layer, with aluminum sometimes available as a costly alternative. This material is laminated to the plywood to protect it from moisture and abrasion and to provide a smart appearance. Unfortunately, extremes of temperature and rough handling can cause plastic to crack or de-laminate. Some manufacturers, such as Gold Star Systems, offer fiberglass-coated plywood as an alternative to plastic to avoid these problems. It is available in several colors like the plastic and is better looking as well as being more durable. Fiberglass-coated plywood is usually a bit more expensive than the plastic-laminated plywood, but less expensive than an outer layer of aluminum.

The aluminum edging is an important part of flight case construction. Ideally, the plywood panels should fit into a groove in the edging, supported on both sides. This is much stronger than edging that supports the plywood only on the outside. Edging around the opening of the case lid should fit together with a tongue-and-groove design when closed. This prevents the case lid from being knocked out of alignment during transport and helps to seal the case against weather, dust, etc.

Some manufacturers use glue and staple construction when putting flight cases together. Rivets are stronger and allow the case to be dismantled if a panel needs replacement. A strong, piano-style hinge should be used for the case lid. Recessed handles and latches are sturdier than surface-mounted hardware and less likely to be damaged during transport.

Very important for large, heavy flight cases is the size and quality of wheels used. Small wheels tend to get stuck in cracks between pavement slabs and do not roll well on rough surfaces or even on thick carpet. They also tend to break or wear out faster than large wheels, since they are not designed to carry much weight. The better quality, large wheels are usually made of hard rubber. Avoid inexpensive wheels or hard plastic wheels that can shatter due to over-loading, rough use or extreme temperatures. Caster wheels that swivel are particularly susceptible to wear under heavy loads or rough use. If they are not top quality, they will soon begin to wobble, eventually becoming so loose that the ball bearings fall out. Any case bulky or heavy enough to require wheels should have the best ones you can get.

Flight cases should be lined inside to absorb bumps and protect against scratches. If a case contains more than one drum, it should be solidly partitioned. Lining materials most commonly used are Ozite carpeting and different grades of foam rubber. The carpeting material is useful for hardware compartments and other areas where scratch protection is more important than shock absorption. Avoid the softer, cheaper grades of foam. They will tear easily and they compress too much under the weight of drum equipment, lowering their shock absorption capability. Insist on harder, high quality foam that will resist tearing and will properly cushion the drums or cymbals.

Roadrunner hard fiber cases, showing detail of riveted construction. *(Courtesy of Roadrunner Cases.)*

If you travel extensively and always have a road crew, one or two large flight cases will keep all your equipment together and protected. If you transport your equipment yourself by car, large cases are not practical. Smaller, individual flight cases will be more likely to fit in your car and you will be able to lift each case by yourself. If the size, weight and cost of flight cases for your complete drumset is prohibitive, you may wish to buy them for only the more delicate components of the drumset (such as your snare drum or your cymbals), while using lighter and less expensive cases for the other equipment. A good case manufacturer will work with you to design flight cases to suit your requirements.

The medium level of protection is provided by cases made of molded plastic, riveted plastic or hard fiber. Examples of these are available ready made from a number of manufacturers. In comparison to flight cases, they are lighter and less expensive, although the better ones are not cheap. Usually these cases are made to fit individual drums, although "trap" cases are available that will hold a snare drum, cymbals and hardware in separate compartments. Except for the largest trap cases (that are usually fitted with

Impact molded plastic cases. Notice Velcro strap closure instead of buckles. *(Courtesy of Impact.)*

caster wheels), one person can lift and carry this type of case without much difficulty. For these large cases, the earlier comments about size and quality of wheels are just as important as for flight cases.

Molded plastic cases, as their name implies, are made of thick plastic material. The lid telescopes onto the body of the case and is held in place by straps and buckles. Being plastic, they are very water and abrasion-resistant and quite strong for their weight. Examples often come with no lining, although there are molded plastic cymbal cases with padding available, such as the Zildjian Cymbal Safe. They are generally stronger than fiber cases, but more expensive. Due to the high cost of producing molds, they are available in a limited range of sizes. The main concern about any plastic cases is their ability to withstand temperature extremes. Some plastics warp out of shape after being left in a car during hot weather and some become brittle when exposed to intense cold. If this is likely to be a concern for you, you should question the manufacturer before buying.

Fiber cases are made from thin, hard fiber board, like a thin sheet of cardboard, but stronger. Some have a smooth finish on the outside that makes them slightly more weather resistant. They are constructed by cutting and riveting pieces of fiber into the desired size and shape. A wide range of sizes is available. Like molded plastic cases, the lid telescopes onto the body of the case and is held in place by straps and buckles. Fiber cases are available in foam lined or unlined models. Some have metal corners to minimize wear and all should have metal "feet" to keep the case from resting directly on wet ground.

Fiber cases can last for years if not abused but there is a wide range of quality available. In comparison to flight cases or molded plastic cases, the bump protection, abrasion resistance and weather resistance of fiber cases is low. They are far more protective than soft cases, but the material has its limitations. You should take care in stacking fiber cases on top of each other. Better examples have metal or reinforced handles. Cheaper examples use inexpensive, plastic handles with no reinforcement. Cheaper handles usually last only a short time on the heavier cases before they break and must be replaced by a luggage repair shop.

As with their quality, the price of fiber cases varies. Compare different fiber cases and consider quality as well as price before choosing.

Riveted plastic cases are constructed in the same manner as fiber cases. Instead of hard fiber, they are made from sheets of thin, flexible plastic material. This provides better weather resistance and abrasion resistance than fiber. No exterior treatment is necessary to improve their durability and their longer lasting material offsets their slightly higher initial cost. A wide range of sizes is available, but not many case manufacturers offer this type of case. One example is the Titan series made by Roadrunner Cases. Titan cases are made from a polyethylene plastic that resists extremes of temperatures. They are available with or without foam lining. As with fiber, when you are shopping for riveted plastic cases, look for good quality, sturdy handles, straps, buckles, etc.

Soft cases provide low level protection. They are available ready made from many manufacturers. The terms "cover" or "bag" are often used to describe them, indicating that they do not provide the serious protection of hard cases. They are light weight and add very little bulk to the equipment they contain. Their price range varies depending on quality of materials and construction.

Soft cases are made of vinyl, various fabrics and leather. Available in a wide range of sizes, they are made for individual drums, sets of cymbals, hardware or sticks. The material is cut and sewn to the desired shape and size with zipper closures and attached handles. Cheaper versions are not lined or padded. The most expensive are often foam padded and lined with soft material. Even the best of these cases do not offer adequate shock absorption for rough handling or extensive travel. They are a light weight and sometimes inexpensive way of covering the equipment, giving it some weather protection and scratch protection and making it easier to transport.

The cheapest soft cases are quite inexpensive. Foam padded versions are more costly and soft leather cases often cost more than good quality hard cases. To ascertain quality, the important areas to examine are the seams, zippers and handles. Other than tearing the material, these are the three areas most likely to fail if the soft case is not well constructed. If you store your drums for any length of time in soft cases made of vinyl, remember that this material is non-porous and moisture in the air could condense inside and cause rust problems. This may or may not be likely, depending on conditions of storage. Alternately, if you transport your drumset in soft cases, the non-porous nature of vinyl provides the best weather protection of the soft case designs.

Care and Maintenance

Keeping your cases in good shape is a relatively simple procedure. Inspecting them periodically will reveal any wear or damage that requires attention. Cases are designed to take punishment that would otherwise damage your drumset. A little time and attention to the following tips will make them last longer and do a better job.

The exterior of a flight case is easily cleaned with a sponge, warm water and soap (such as dishwashing liquid). Avoid getting the inside of the case wet unless the lining also requires cleaning. Foam padding or carpet lining will take a while to dry and water may seep into the plywood. A hair dryer set on low heat can help dry out the foam or carpet inside if cleaning is necessary. Metal edging and hardware can be cleaned and brightened with metal polish, which will also work on the outer layer of aluminum-sheathed cases. Plastic or fiberglass outer layers will benefit from occasional applications of silicone protectants such as Armor All, which will keep them looking shiny and new.

Be sure to lubricate the hinges, locking latches and caster wheels regularly. Rough use can damage plywood panels and loosen rivets. Torn or missing interior padding material can lead to equipment damage. Have any necessary repairs made to the cases as soon as possible.

Molded or riveted plastic cases can also be cleaned with soap and water. Applications of Armor All or similar silicone liquid will keep them shiny and retard the damage that ultra-violet light and air pollution cause to plastic materials. Use metal polish on any metal hardware and have worn or broken straps, buckles or handles replaced at a luggage repair shop.

Inspect plastic cases for cracks. These can sometimes be fixed with fiberglass repair kits available at automotive stores. If the cases are not lined, foam rubber padding can be glued inside them to improve their shock absorption capability. First check to see that there is adequate clearance for the foam between the case and the equipment it contains. Foam can be glued in place with contact cement but it is wise to check with the manufacturer first to be sure that the glue will not damage the plastic case material.

Hard fiber cases can be wiped with soap and water if necessary, but the fiber will absorb water, so use only a damp sponge or cloth and allow the cases to dry thoroughly before use. Metal polish will keep any metal hardware rust-free and shiny. Check fiber cases for tears or holes. Sharp objects can punch through a fiber case and abrasion will wear out the edges if they are treated roughly. This type of damage can be fixed with a fiberglass repair it. Inspect handles, straps and buckles for wear or damage and replace or repair as necessary. Lubricate caster wheels on trap cases or hardware boxes.

Even the fiber cases with glossy finishes are not very water resistant. You can improve the weather and abrasion resistance of this material by spraying or brush coating the exterior of the case with two or more coats of clear polyurethane, varnish or similar sealant. The first coat will be partially absorbed by the fiber, so at least two coats are necessary for a good job. This also leaves the case with a shiny, attractive finish.

If your fiber cases are unlined, you can improve their shock absorption capability by lining them with foam rubber as described for plastic cases. With either type of case, if there is insufficient clearance to completely line the interior, foam can be glued to the bottom and or the ends of the case. These are the areas where the weight of the equipment is most likely to rest and where the lining is most needed. The harder, stiffer grades of foam offer the best padding and are the ones least likely to tear.

Vinyl and fabric soft cases can usually be hand washed in a sink or laundry tub and allowed to dry thoroughly before use. Before washing a fabric case, check the type of material to determine whether it is likely to shrink. Generally, there is more danger of shrinkage in natural fibers than synthetic fibers. When dry, vinyl soft cases can be wiped with Armor All or other silicone liquid to prevent the material from drying out and cracking. Fabric cases might benefit from an application of a stain resistant spray coating such as Scotchguard. Leather cases can be cleaned with saddle soap or other quality leather cleaner and conditioner.

Tears and ripped seams in soft cases can sometimes be patched or re-sewn and zippers can be replaced if they break. Be sure to inspect the area where the handles are attached to the case. This area receives the most stress when the case is carried.

Mark your cases with your name, address and phone number. This is especially important if your drumset is transported by commercial carrier or loaded in a band vehicle with lots of other equipment. Luggage tags, paint, self-adhesive label tape, your own decals or stickers or a combination of these things will work. If other people will be handling your cases, a few FRAGILE stickers should be used.

Choosing Cases

As with your choice of drums, cymbals, hardware, heads, sticks, etc., you should buy the best cases you can afford for your application. The following guidelines are designed to help you determine the level of protection you need. They will also help you evaluate the ratio of cost vs. protection level for each type of case.

The one soft case recommended for any drummer is the stick bag. Using a stick bag is the simplest way to keep your sticks, brushes and mallets organized and within easy reach when you are performing. There are variations in size and design but a stick bag is basically a carrying case that opens up and hangs from your floor tom. The sticks, brushes and mallets are held in open pockets so you can grab whatever you need as you play. When the performance is over, the stick bag zips up and packs in your hardware case. Most good stick bags have at least one closed accessory pocket to hold your drum tuning key and a small selection of other tools or spare parts.

Stick bags have become so popular that there has been some serious thought put into their design. Pro-Mark's stick bags, for example, have a Quick Zip feature that does not require you to fit the ends of the zipper together when closing the bag. They zip closed from the top to the bottom instead of the opposite direction. This eliminates the gap at the top where the zipper usually ends, preventing sticks from falling out if the bag is turned upside down while closed. Several bags are fitted with adjustable shoulder straps to make carrying easier and there are large capacity bags that will hold a larger number of sticks, brushes and mallets. The Kevin Roadbag sold by Rimshot America has two large interior pockets behind the stick pockets to hold sheet music or drum instruction books. Instead of the usual straps, it uses an elastic cord to secure the bag to the floor tom. Many of the better stick bags are padded with foam or lined with soft material to protect the contents from damage during transport. There are stick bags in several sizes, different materials and various price ranges. It is worth shopping around to find the features you need.

Other soft cases are useful for the drummer on a tight budget. Any case is better than none and the cheaper soft cases provide some protection for a relatively small cash outlay. If money is the limiting factor, avoid the more expensive soft cases. Their higher cost might buy a set of hard cases that would offer more protection. The soft leather and expensive padded fabric cases are a logical choice only for the drummer who can afford hard cases but wants the light weight and minimal bulk of a soft case for occasional transport. In general, soft cases are adequate protection for the drummer who just wants to store his or her drums safely at home. If you rarely move your drumset and always carry it yourself, soft cases are the minimum level of protection you need.

Molded or riveted plastic and hard fiber cases provide more protection than soft cases with a bit more additional weight, bulk and (sometimes, but not always) cost. The more handling your drumset receives, the more potential damage it is subjected to. If you transport your drums on a regular basis but still carry them yourself, hard fiber or plastic cases offer the minimum level of protection you need.

Going "on the road" is hard on a drumset and hard on its cases. Even if you carry your own equipment, you will find that flight cases are more durable than other types. Their added weight and bulk is the major disadvantage for drummers who must do their own carrying, but the use of caster wheels can minimize this problem. Flight cases should be seriously considered by drummers who do much touring. As mentioned previously, using flight cases for your snare drum, cymbals or other delicate items along with plastic or fiber cases for the rest is a good compromise. If your drumset must travel by commercial carrier or if it is handled by a road crew, you should consider nothing but flight cases. No other case will withstand such rough treatment over prolonged periods.

If you use your own vehicle to transport a drumset, be certain that the cases you choose will fit in it. Do some measuring or try fitting the cases before you buy.

If you have an expensive drumset and want serious protection for it, obtain competitive price quotes for the various styles of cases available to you. Weigh the cost against the level of protection offered. Then consider the life expectancy of the case. Better quality, stronger cases may last as long as two or three sets of cheaper, flimsy cases, making them a better bargain in the long run. During their service life, they will also do a better job of protecting your drumset. Do not let your equipment go unprotected.

Setting Up the Drumset

The acoustic drumset is a relatively new concept. At the beginning of the twentieth century, most bands used two drummers: a snare drummer and a bass drummer. These different functions are still handled by separate musicians in most symphony orchestras. The invention of reliable bass drum pedals allowed one drummer to play both bass drum and snare drum. This started the evolution of the drumset.

The popular music drummers of that time were expected to play a number of "traps" such as cymbals, tom-toms, cow bells, wood blocks, temple blocks, xylophones, etc., in addition to the bass drum and snare drum. They could buy all these components separately, but it was not until some time in the 1920s that drum manufacturers began to sell matched sets of drums with provision for mounting various accessories in convenient locations.

The whole idea of a drumset was to allow the drummer to sit in one place and have access to all his or her traps. Old movies and old photographs show some of the strange looking (to modern eyes) set-ups that were used. There was a gradual standardization of component type, size and location over the years, eventually leading to the kind of drumset configurations we are now accustomed to.

The drumset is still evolving in response to changes in popular music, but it remains a collection of percussion instruments grouped together for easy access by one seated individual. If your drumset is not providing that easy access with all the technological advances in hardware over the years, it is time for you to give the problem some serious consideration.

Many drum teachers do not spend time teaching their students how to set up (or tune) their equipment. Other musicians often have little understanding of how crucial it is for drummers to have everything set up just the way they want it.

Drum equipment is complex and setting up your drumset is comparable to a guitar player assembling his or her guitar from its component pieces every time there is a performance. Setting up without an understanding of certain concepts can result in a sub-standard performance. If you are fighting your equipment, you cannot concentrate on playing. Straining to reach drums or cymbals slows you down and results in unnecessary fatigue.

Setting up correctly means not having to think about where each component of the set is. It allows you to concentrate on your playing. By locating your equipment where it is most accessible, speed is maximized and fatigue is minimized.

It is impossible to make hard and fast rules about "right" and "wrong" ways to set up equipment. All individuals and body dimensions are different. Also, the sizes and configurations of drumsets are different. However, certain principles should be taken into account and certain mechanical and design limitations of the equipment must be considered.

To avoid repetition, certain instructions in this section are worded for right-handed drummers. Left-handed drummers who wish to play left-handed set-ups should reverse these instructions. Other alternatives are to learn to play right-handed or ambidexterously on a right-handed drumset. If you play primarily left-handed on a right-handed drumset, you will want to mount your hi-hat cymbals lower than a right-handed drummer would find convenient. You may also find it more comfortable to place your ride cymbal on your left. Otherwise, read on.

The first variable to be considered when setting up your drumset is your body. How long are your arms and legs? Do you hold your drumsticks in the matched or traditional grip? If you try to fit your body to your equipment instead of the other way around, you are asking for both physical problems and performance problems. Many drummers suffer from back pain due to bad posture at the drumset. Sitting on a back-less stool with your feet operating pedals puts a lot of strain on your spine. Bending and stretching at odd angles to reach parts of the set can cause further aches and pains.

The ideal set-up is one where you can sit comfortably, reach anything easily and play with as little wasted motion as possible. The components of the drumset that are used most often should be in the most convenient locations. Items that are used less often can be placed farther away or in less convenient locations.

It is not always possible to achieve this, but if we use our bodies as a starting point and build the drumset around them, we are moving in the right direction. This is how the first drumsets were developed, resulting in the now traditional placement of modern drumset components.

Setting up your drumset on a carpeted surface protects the shell of the bass drum from being scratched on dirty or rough floors. It also provides a non-slippery, textured surface to keep your bass drum and hi-hat from sliding away from you as you play. If you carry your own piece of carpet, you can mark the location of drums and stands on it to help duplicate a precise set-up each time. A ready made version of this is the Gig Rug, made by the L.T. Lug Lock company. It is a carpet designed for drumsets with a built-in barrier to keep your bass drum from sliding.

The first piece of equipment to set up is the throne. It is necessary to have a firm foundation to sit on. Ideally, your throne should not wobble at all. Set the height so that you can sit comfortably. Some drummers like to sit low while others prefer to sit high. If you have long legs, you should not sit too low. If your legs are short, do not sit so high that your legs are stretched out with your feet straining to reach the pedals. A good mid-point is where your back is straight and your thighs are approximately horizontal, putting your knees at the same height as your hips. Start with your throne at this height and experiment with slightly more or less height until you find the most comfortable position.

Place your feet just slightly forward of an imaginary vertical line drawn from your knees to the floor. This permits you to use your feet on the pedals in both the heel up and heel down manner. If your feet are too far in front of you, you will not have power when you need it. If they are tucked in behind your knees, you will not be able to execute soft passages comfortably by keeping your heel down and pivoting your foot at the ankle. Your knees should be spread apart comfortably.

Your arms should hang relaxed, straight down from shoulder to elbow. Your elbows should be at your sides, but not touching your sides, not out ahead of your body and not behind an imaginary line drawn straight down from the shoulder. Your arms should bend straight forward at the elbow. With the sticks in your hands, you should be able to sit relaxed and comfortably in this position. The pedals and other components of the drumset should be within easy reach (unless you play a particularly large, elaborate drumset).

The equipment must be built around this seating position. To start with, let us assume that you have a four- or five-piece drumset. After learning the basic set-up, there will be some suggestions for those of you with larger sets.

After the throne, always start by setting up the bass drum. The rest of the drumset is built around it and in some cases mounts on it. Place the bass drum on the floor with the spurs extended evenly on each side. If the spur height is uneven, it alters the angle of the bass drum and changes the position of toms or cymbals that may be mounted on it. Spur height should be set to raise the resonator side counterhoop of the bass drum slightly off the floor. This permits the drum to resonate freely and puts the weight on the spurs, stopping any side-to-side wobble and preventing the drum from sliding forward as it is played.

Next, lift the batter side counterhoop slightly and slide the bass drum pedal into position. Fasten it firmly in place on the counterhoop, avoiding excessive tightening that might damage the counterhoop. Adjust the height of the pedal beater rod so that the beater strikes the batter head near the center of the drum. Experiment with center, slightly above and slightly below center to get the sound and feel you like. Locate your throne so that your right foot rests comfortably on the bass drum pedal when you are in the previously described seating position. You may want to vary the angle of your seating position relative to the batter head of the drum. Facing the drum directly may put your foot at an odd angle on the pedal footboard.

The next two components to set up are the hi-hat and the snare drum. Set the tripod base of the hi-hat stand where your left foot falls when you're sitting comfortably with your knees apart. Position it so that your foot is at a comfortable angle when it rests on the footboard. Now set the height of the stand as high as it will adjust and put the cymbals in place. We will use this as a starting point and experiment with lower heights when the snare drum has been placed in position.

Put the base of the snare drum stand on the floor between the two pedals. Set the snare drum on the stand so that you can reach the snare throw-off lever without fumbling for it. Adjust the height of the snare drum stand so that the batter head is right underneath the height that you hold the tips of your drumsticks while in the described seated position. This will probably be higher than your knees but no higher than your waist. If the drum is too high, you will waste motion lifting your whole arm to play it. If it is too low, you will strike your legs while trying to hit rim shots. Ideally, this drum should be played with the sticks almost parallel to the head when your arms are in a relaxed position. Too little or too much height makes this difficult.

Next, you must adjust the angle of the snare drum. Matched grip players usually prefer the drum flat or tilting slightly toward them or directly away from them. This is because matched grip allows you to play with the same muscular action at the same angle with both hands.

The right-handed traditional grip player uses a grip that was developed to accommodate a marching drum hanging from a sling over the drummer's right shoulder. The marching drum rested on the left leg with the batter head slanted down roughly from left to right (from the drummer's viewpoint).

If you use traditional grip on the drumset, you will find it easiest to play directly off the head and hit rim shots with your left hand if you duplicate the angle for which the grip was developed. Experiment with different degrees of angle with the highest part of the counterhoop located where your left stick crosses it when held in a relaxed position. The drum should slope down to your right and slightly away from you. A small variation of this angle can make things much easier or much more difficult. It may take a lot of experimentation to get it right.

The snare drum should sit at your chosen height and angle so that the tips of your drumsticks rest naturally near the center of the drumhead. Do not place it too close to yourself or you will be leaning backwards to play it. Do not place it too far away or you will be reaching for it. If you have to reach for your snare drum, you will have trouble reaching a tom that is placed beyond it.

When the snare drum is in place, go back to the hi-hat. If you cross your right hand over your left to play the hi-hat cymbals (as most right-handed drummers do), your hi-hat cymbals must be close enough to reach without leaning your body to the left. They must also be high enough above the snare drum to allow you to play the snare drum with your left hand while your right hand plays the hi-hat cymbals. Move the hi-hat stand as close to the snare drum as is necessary to permit access to the cymbals. Then start experimenting with the height of the hi-hat cymbals until you have found the optimum position. If you play loudly most of the time, you will want to raise your left hand high for back beats on the snare drum and you will want to play with the shank or shoulder of the drumstick on the edge of the hi-hat cymbals for maximum volume. Use as much height as is necessary to accomplish this. If you are a softer player, you will want to use the tip of your right drumstick, sometimes at a downward angle, on the bow of the top hi-hat cymbal for the softest effect. In order to achieve this, less height for the hi-hat cymbals will allow you to play them from a more "on top" position.

Now adjust the gap between the top and bottom hi-hat cymbals by securing the hi-hat clutch at the desired height on the pull rod. The larger the gap, the farther your foot must push the pedal to bring the cymbals together. Individual tastes vary, but if you want to get sufficient volume and a clear "chick" sound when operating the pedal, start with the cymbals the width of two fingers apart and experiment from there. If the "chick" sound is not clear, try using the adjuster under the bottom cymbal to tilt this cymbal slightly. This causes the cymbals to come together off center, preventing air lock and muffled sound. Experiment with more or less tilt to get the effect you want.

Next come the toms. Place the floor tom to your right, beside your right leg. It should be close enough to reach with your left drumstick without leaning your body or twisting your spine very much. The height of the floor tom should be roughly the same as your snare drum so you do not have to change your angle of attack with the drumsticks when moving from one drum to the other. It is best to have the batter head flat or tilted to face you slightly. The ideal is to be able to play directly off the head while maintaining a relaxed position.

Five-piece drumsets usually mount the two smaller toms on a tom holder connected to the shell of the bass drum. These toms are farther away from you, so the ideal position for them is as close as possible to avoid reaching very far. The smallest tom is usually mounted on the left (from the drummer's perspective), in front of the snare drum. The larger tom is placed on the right, in front of the floor tom. This creates a descending range of pitch from left to right, which is comfortable for the right-handed drummer who leads most often with his or her right hand. It is not necessary to place the drums in this order. You may find it interesting to reverse them and see how it affects your playing style.

Tom holders mounted on the bass drum have built-in positioning limitations depending on the diameter of the bass drumshell and the depth of the toms. Minimum height adjustment leaves the toms almost resting on the shell of the bass drum. If you use a large diameter bass drum and your snare drum and floor tom are not set very high, this may leave your mounted toms far above the height of the snare drum and floor tom. The opposite problem is rarely encountered. Maximum height on modern tom holders is usually adequate.

To experience the effect that tom height and angle can have on play- ing technique, mount your small toms with their batter heads horizontal at the same height as your snare drum and floor tom. As you move your drumsticks from the snare drum to the mounted toms, observe the amount of arm and or body movement this requires. Now raise the height of the mounted toms two inches and tilt them so that their batter heads face you slightly. Move your sticks from snare drum to mounted toms again and notice the reduction in arm/body movement required. This translates into more speed, more power and less fatigue over the course of a performance. Mounted toms are farther away than your snare drum or floor tom. This slight difference in height and angle brings them closer.

Don't overdo it, however. If the mounted toms are tilted too sharply towards you, you will have to change your angle of attack with the sticks when moving from snare drum or floor tom to mounted toms or vice versa. The same thing happens when you mount your toms high above your snare drum. When moving from one drum to another, very small differences in positioning can affect the fluidity of your playing, which is very important for a really musical performance. One reason for avoiding extended depth tom shells is that their depth often necessitates this extreme difference in positioning of drum heights and angles.

Another thing to consider when setting up mounted toms is their location in relation to each other. Most modern tom holders have a provision for moving the toms closer together or farther apart. If your drumming style requires fast moves from one drum to another, the logical thing to do is reduce the distance between drums as much as is practical. Keeping the toms close together also allows the cymbals to be placed closer to you for easy access. The standard five-piece drumset necessitates cymbals placed above the drums. The higher and farther away the cymbals are, the more time and effort it takes to reach them. This makes your work more difficult.

A right-handed drummer will want the ride cymbal on the right side of the drumset (from his or her point of view) where it is easily accessible to the right hand. The position of a ride cymbal is more critical than a crash cymbal because the ride cymbal is usually played consistently when it is played, while a crash cymbal is only struck intermittently. The best position for the ride cymbal is on the drummer's right (but not too far to the right) and as low as the height of a mounted tom or even lower. This eliminates the fatigue of holding your right arm up for extended periods as you play the ride cymbal. Since it is one of the most frequently used parts of the drumset (except for certain styles of rock, where the hi-hat gets much more use than the ride cymbal), it should be located as closely and comfortably as possible.

If you use a four-piece drumset, this problem can be solved easily by placing your ride cymbal where the larger of the two toms is usually mounted on a five-piece drumset. When four-piece drumsets were the standard, basic drumset, there was often a cymbal holder mounted on the bass drumshell in that position. If you have a five-piece set, there are a couple of ways to get your ride cymbal into this position. One way is to place it on a stand to the right of your larger mounted tom, just beyond your floor tom and as low as possible. If this is not comfortable enough, you can move your mounted toms onto a floor stand to the left of your bass drum and mount the ride cymbal where the larger of the toms used to be. If you dislike floor stands for toms, you can use the left side of the bass-drum-mounted tom holder for the larger tom and a separate clamp mount to the left of that, which attaches the smaller tom to a cymbal stand or other piece of hardware.

Crash cymbals can be placed in slightly less convenient areas because they are not struck as frequently. The main considerations are that they must be relatively easy to reach and they must not interfere with your access to other drums, the ride cymbal or the hi-hat. The most common position for a crash cymbal is on a floor stand (near the hi-hat and the smallest mounted tom) to your left. A cymbal in this position must be close enough to be reached by your right hand, which sometimes dictates the use of a boom cymbal stand.

Another position for a crash cymbal is on a floor stand to the right of your floor tom, above the ride cymbal. For splash cymbals or other small crashes, try a shell-mounted or counterhoop-mounted holder on the bass drum so that the cymbal is between the two mounted toms, just beyond them. Some types of bass drum mounted tom holders have provision for mounting a small cymbal in this location.

Boom cymbal stands permit you to place a cymbal close enough when there is no room for the base of a cymbal stand that close. When you are using a boom stand, you can locate a cymbal above another cymbal or drum, high enough that it does not restrict your access to the lower item. This is particularly useful when trying to place a cymbal on one side of the drumset so that it is close enough to be struck by the opposite hand. Always turn the base of a boom stand so that one of the legs extends in the same direction as the boom. This provides more stability to help prevent the stand from tipping over when you hit the cymbal.

When you are setting up a drumset with more than five drums, the same basic principles apply. Within the limitations of space and the hardware's range of adjustment, try to fit the drums to your body rather than making your body fit the drums. Double bass drumsets present a special problem of placing the hi-hat close enough to the snare drum to allow the right hand to cross over and reach the hi-hat cymbals. The hi-hat stand is usually placed to the left of the left bass drum pedal, putting it out of comfortable reach of your right hand. Folding up the hi-hat stand tripod and using a clamp to secure the hi-hat stand to the counterhoop of the left bass drum brings it closer. It can thus be placed immediately to the left of the left bass drum pedal instad of far to the left. If you use two bass drums all the time, a legless hi-hat stand designed for this purpose is the best choice. If you use several mounted toms, you may encounter interference between the hi-hat cymbals and the tom mounted farthest to the left. Situations like this call for a compromise, moving one or both components to heights and angles where they do not collide and are still accessible.

More than one floor tom can also be awkward, especially if they are both of large diameters (such as 16″ and 18″). The larger floor tom is usually adjusted to the same height as the smaller one and placed behind it (from the audience point of view). This maintains the downward pitch sweep of tom sounds from the drummer's left to his or her right. Unfortunately, in order to strike the larger floor tom, you must twist your upper body around substantially. If you find this awkward, try placing one of the floor toms beside your left leg instead. It is much more accessible in that location.

Common sense dictates that you should limit the number of components in your drumset to what you can reach comfortably. A piece of equipment is of no value if you cannot get at it when you need it. Limiting your equipment also makes it easier to transport and takes up less room on a crowded stage. After several years of larger and more elaborate drumsets, it is interesting to note a trend among many professional drummers back to more basic four- and five-piece drumsets. You may find that using a smaller set-up forces you to think and play more creatively on the drums and cymbals that you have available.

These general instructions should be regarded as a starting point for your experimentation. During your practice sessions, try adjusting one component at a time by small increments. Keep your mind open to new ideas, as new hardware is being introduced all the time to make it easier to achieve ideal set-ups. Make adjustments based on what feels better and is easier to play. Do not set up your drumset in an unplayable position just because it seems to look good.

Drumset Spare Parts
and Repair Kit

Put together a spare parts and repair kit for your drumset. Depending on your situation, you may want to keep most of this equipment at home or take it with you while performing.

The specific requirements of your drumset will determine some of the items you will need. The following suggestions, combined with careful reading of earlier sections of this book, will give you some ideas. Remember that parts never seem to break or disappear when you are within easy reach of a well stocked music store. Things tend to go wrong at the worst possible moment, so it is worth buying most of these items for future use rather than needing them when the stores are closed or unavailable.

An adequate supply of spare drumsticks, brushes and mallets is necessary. A small towel to keep your hands free of perspiration while performing is very useful. Spare drumheads for each drum (especially batter side heads) are a must. Also include a spare snare-side head for your snare drum, since this head is extra-thin and easily damaged. Carry a small block of paraffin wax for the bearing edge of shells when changing heads.

Different types of bass drum beaters for different acoustic conditions and volume levels, a spare bass drum pedal strap and spring and a spare hi-hat clutch can save the day. Extra muffling materials, spare tension rods and washers, plastic tubing and felt washers for cymbal stands, spare wing nuts and rubber feet are often needed. A spare set of snares is good insurance. Be sure to have plenty of snare cord, tape or plastic strips (depending on how your snares are attached to the drum).

Maintenance items include soft, clean cloths, cotton swabs and a soft bristle brush for cleaning and polishing, metal polish, cymbal polish, wax for exterior finishes and grease and oil for lubrication. Tools include spare drum tuning keys, Allen wrenches, pliers and screwdrivers or nut drivers.

Also keep a copy of *The Drumset Owner's Manual* in your kit for instructions on maintenance procedures.

Surprisingly, except for the spare drumheads, you can get all the spare parts and repair equipment needed for an extended tour into a large briefcase. Start building your own spare parts and repair kit piece by piece. Soon, you will be able to handle most emergencies and routine maintenance from the supplies you have on hand. Check your stock at regular intervals and replenish the items that are in short supply.

Index